BEASTLY KNITS

BEASTLY KNITS

by Lalla Ward

Technical Advice by
Anni Bowes

ST MARTIN'S PRESS · NEW YORK

Photography by Colin Thomas
Cover and book design by Richard Brown Associates
Knitted sweaters by Anni Bowes
Illustrations by Lalla Ward

ISBN 0–312–07041–1

Published in Great Britain in 1985
by Sidgwick & Jackson Limited

First U.S. edition
10 9 8 7 6 5 4 3 2 1

Typeset by Rapidset and Design Ltd., London WC1
Printed in Italy by New Interlitho SpA Milan

TO ALL THE KNITS I KNOW,
AND THE THREE BEASTS IN MY LIFE

I would especially like to thank my mother for allowing me to use the wonderful carved wooden animals from the Lady Bangor Private Fairground Collection for the photographs in this book.

Special thanks, too, to Anni Bowes for working so hard knitting every one of these twenty-nine sweaters in an unbelievably short time and for her endless encouragement and advice.

Thank you to my parents and all my friends and their children for giving up their time to come and model my Beastly Knits so beautifully. And I would like to thank the following for all their help and kindness:
Colin Thomas, Richard Brown, Heather Jeeves
Jaeger Hand Knitting Ltd
Rosemary King
Keith Nichols at Texere Yarns
Stephen Grant and Suzanne Russell at Yarnworks
Nina Miklin
Keith Roberts at Patricia Roberts Knitting Ltd

IMPORTANT NOTICE
CORRECTIONS

Page 18 Third column, fourth line from top should read:
Row 102

Page 58 **Start Pattern.** The last three lines should read:
Adjust row counter to Row 117.
Row 118-148: Work in St. st.

Page 62 **Start Pattern.** The last three lines should read:
Adjust row counter to Row 146.
Row 147-155: Work in St. st.

Page 62 **Neck Shaping.** The instructions should read as follows:
Row 156: P73, P2tog. Join new colour A and P2tog. P73.
Row 157: K74sts on both sides of neck.
Row 158: P72, P2tog. On other side of neck P2tog. P72.
Row 159: K73sts on both sides of neck.
Row 160-199: Continue to dec. one st. at neck edge of every P row (48sts).

CONTENTS

THE NATURE OF THE BEAST

This chapter contains all the basic technical information you will need in order to tackle a Beastly Knit. I'm assuming that you already know how to knit and purl; in addition you will need to know the following:

YARNS

I felt that it was up to me to investigate all the many colours and yarns available and I've chosen the ones that I, personally, liked best. I've used wonderful silk/cotton mixtures, alpaca, angora, cotton, mohair and a silk/wool mixture. All of these yarns knit as 4-ply and if you want to be more economical you can substitute your own choice of yarn. I do suggest that you leave the colours of the Beasts as specified – a green flamingo would look rather bizarre, likewise a purple and pink panda, but do by all means choose your own favourite colour for the backgrounds as long as you go for a colour that contrasts well with the Beast. For instance, white as a background for the Polar Bear might make all your hard work rather a wasted effort.

SIZING

As you can see from the photographs, I have purposely chosen to make these Beastly Knits loose rather than tight fitting in order to give space to the designs, and for that reason you will be unable to make them any smaller than specified. If you are going to take the time to make one of these sweaters for say, a small child, it's nice to know that he or she won't grow out of it too quickly.

All of these Beastly Knits can be made in larger sizes, simply by measuring the person for whom you are making the sweater, referring to the tension instructions given with each pattern and increasing the number of stitches accordingly. For example, if the pattern given is for 120 stitches and you wish to increase it by ten stitches you can increase five stitches on either side [and obviously increase five stitches either side on the back of the sweater] only if the particular design of the Beast is in the centre of the sweater. If it is one of those designs which crosses a side seam and continues on the back of the sweater, like, for example the Polar Bear, you will have to add your ten extra stitches on the opposite side, both front and back, and re-centre the neckline, both front and back. Remember, too, that because you have re-centred the neckline, you will have to cast off five extra stitches on each shoulder-shaping.

To increase the length of the sweater, add extra rows between the ribbing and the start of the design. To increase the sleeve length add the appropriate number of rows at the shoulder end of your work, after completing the specified number of increases.

EQUIPMENT

You will need the following:

Knitting needles. Sizes given in the patterns are in metric with U.S. equivalents in brackets. Below is a table of all the needle sizes used in the book giving the English pre-metric size as well.

METRIC	2¼mm	2¾mm	3mm	3¼mm	3¾mm
U.S.	0	1	2	3	4
ENGLISH (pre-metric)	13	12	11	10	9

A row counter is essential because you will need to know precisely which row you are on when following the graph – don't forget to turn it on one at the end of each row!

A stitch holder is used for the front neck shaping in these patterns.

A crochet hook is used for securing the many loose ends of yarn on the wrong side of your finished work. Don't tie these loose ends in knots. They leave Beastly bumps and tend to come undone.

Glass or plastic headed pins. If you use the ordinary type of pin, you could lose it in the thickness of the work. The coloured heads of the glass or plastic ones are much easier to see.

A tapestry needle, both for sewing up and for the embroidery.
Patience!

TENSION

Before starting to make any of the sweaters you will need to work a tension sample in order to check your individual control over the yarns against that recommended in the pattern. This will ensure that your knitting is the same as the measurements given in each pattern. The yarn used to knit the tension samples for each pattern

9

is always the background yarn, so if you choose a different yarn, it is even more important to check your tension.

If the number of stitches given in the pattern are too wide against the measurement, you are working too loosely. Use a smaller size needle. On the other hand, if they are too narrow, you are working too tightly. Use a larger size needle.

CASTING ON

To avoid loops along the bottom edge of your ribbing, work into the back of each stitch as you cast on. That is, put the right-hand needle through the back of the stitch you have just made, on the left-hand needle. Then make another new stitch and slip it on to the left-hand needle.

SINGLE RIBBING

Ribbing is a combination of knit and purl stitches used to form a neat, stretchable finish to sleeves and waistbands. All the sweaters which have ribbing are worked in single rib, which is one knit stitch, one purl stitch alternately to the end of the row. Unless otherwise stated, always start a new row with a knit stitch.

It is difficult to measure tension on ribbing, but all the ribbing in the sweaters has been worked firmly on the needles. If you tend to knit loosely, use a smaller size needle. Casting off in rib is down loosely to enable the ribbing to stretch, especially over your head.

INCREASING

I have used two ways to increase stitches and you will find an explanation and the appropriate abbreviation at the beginning of the instructions for each pattern.

DECREASING

Again, you will find an explanation with the instructions for each Beastly Knit.

WEAVING

Weaving can be used when you are working a pattern with more than two colours and when yarn is carried over more than five stitches.

1. In a knit row, hold the white yarn as illustrated, in your right hand and the black yarn in your left hand at the back of the work.

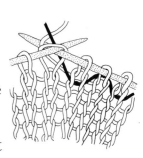

Fig. 1

2. Knit one stitch with the white yarn and at the same time, bring the black yarn under the white yarn. When you are using the black yarn in the pattern, weave the white yarn as described above.

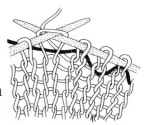

Fig. 2

When working a purl row you will need to hold the white yarn in your right hand and the black yarn in your left hand at the front of the work. Purl one stitch with the white yarn but this time bring the black yarn under the white yarn.

When the black yarn is being used in the pattern, weave the white yarn as described above.

DIVIDING

A variation of weaving is to divide each ball of yarn into the approximate amount required for each block of colour, as specified in the preparation instructions for each Beastly pattern. I have found this method to be a better way of achieving a much neater effect although it is more tiresome to have a lot of Beastly little balls trailing from the back of your work. If you have any cats in the house I strongly recommend that they be shut in another room or you really will find yourself in a dreadful tangle!

When changing to another colour you will need to cross the two colours where they join. In a knit row, across the working colour in front of the new colour and drop the working colour to the back. Knit the next stitch on your left-hand needle with the new colour. On the return purl row the colours will automatically loop together.

When changing to another colour in a purl row, pick up the new colour in front of the working colour and use that new colour to purl the next stitch on your left-hand needle. On the return knit row the colours will automatically loop together.

CASTING OFF

When the instructions tell you to cast off, do so in the appropriate stitch. For example, if the row you would next work is a knit row, then cast off by knitting each stitch first. If the row you would next work is a purl row, then cast off by working in purl stitches.

Should you be casting off in rib, then wind the yarn round to the back of the right-hand needle after a purl stitch prior to lifting the first stitch over the second stitch.

11

EMBROIDERY

I've tried to keep the embroidery as simple as possible, but, as I've explained in the chapter on the Eagle and the Owl, if you are an experienced needleperson you can have a lot of fun adding all sorts of extra details.

You will need stranded embroidery cotton in black and white for most of the patterns. One or two require grey and brown of which any shade will do and I have given some of the animals green or yellow eyes. It's entirely up to you if you particularly want your cat to have green eyes or the rabbit a pink eye, or whatever. Obviously dark colours will show up well on light backgrounds and vice versa. The pigs' nose-rings are in gold metallic thread and the whale's little teeth are in silver lurex.

I find that if you divide the six-stranded cotton in half so that you are using a finer, three-stranded thread you can make your stitches smaller and neater. Be careful not to embroider too tightly or you will lose the elasticity of your knitted background.

You will need to know the following four basic stitches:

Fig. A

Chain stitch (Fig. A)
This is the most useful and I think best follows the shape of a knitted stitch.

Bring your needle through at A. Make a small loop and put the needle in again at A, holding the loop down. Bring the needle up again at B and pull the thread through keeping the loop under the needle point to form your first chain stitch. Repeat, putting the needle in again at B, coming up at C and holding the loop down under the needle point to form your second stitch.

A single chain stitch in white makes a good highlight to an eye, or a bird's nostril.

French knots (Fig. B)
These, too, are useful for highlighting an eye or for cat's whisker-dots.

Bring the thread through at the required place. Hold the thread down with the left thumb. Encircle the needle twice with the thread as in (1). Hold the thread firmly but not too tightly. Put the needle back in close to where the thread first emerged. Pull the thread through and secure for a single knot or continue to the position of the next knot(2).

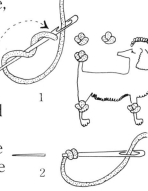

Fig. B

Back stitch (Fig. C)

I've used this stitch occasionally as a simple means of outlining. Bring the thread through on the line you are following. Make a small backward stitch. Bring the needle through again a little in front of your first stitch. Make another stitch, putting your needle in at the point where it first came through.

Fig. C

Overcast stitch (Fig. D)

Lay a thread along the outline you are following, for instance, of the mouse's tail in the Cat and Mouse sweater or the Saddleback Pig's nose-rings. Work small stitches closely over the laid thread, following the line of the design. The stitch looks like a fine cord.

Animal faces (Fig. E)

I've given you variations on how to create Beastly Faces, such as the Tiger face (1), oval eyes as used in the Kangaroo design (2), or round eyes of chain stitch with a French knot in the middle for the birds (3). I've done the claws on the cats and birds in tiny chain stitch with a single back stitch for the sharp tip.

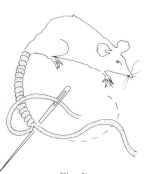

Fig. D

Making up

Before joining up the individual pieces they should be pinned out to shape. This is best achieved by covering a table with a thick cloth or blanket and then a sheet. Use rustproof pins to secure the individual piece carefully, wrong side upwards. Check and correct measurements, taking care not to stretch or distort. Check the yarn manufacturer's instructions given on the ball band before pressing. If it does not recommend pressing, simply cover the pinned out pieces with a damp cloth for a few hours, then remove and allow the pieces to dry completely before unpinning. If you can press the yarn, use a warm iron and a damp cloth or a steam iron. Do not press down hard or you will squash and distort the stitches. Simply holding the steam iron just above the knitting and moving it back and forth so that the steam penetrates the yarn is sometimes sufficient for delicate yarns such as mohair or angora. *Do not press the ribbing.* Ensure the work is completely dry before carefully removing the pins and sewing up. Begin sewing up the sweater, right sides facing, by pinning the shoulder seams together, making sure that the ribbing at the neck edge is even. Sew from shoulder edge to neck edge using back stitch. Sew the ribbing using over

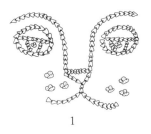

1

2

3

Fig. E

13

stitch, similar to overcast stitch, otherwise you will make a ridge.

Next find the centre of the sleeve top by folding it in half. With right sides facing, place the centre of the sleeve on the shoulder seam and pin from there outwards on both sides. When sewing a sleeve into a sweater with a central design on the front, make sure your second sleeve seam measures exactly the same as the other sleeve seam. When sewing a sleeve into a sweater where the design goes under one arm, sew this sleeve in first, so that you do not sew over the top edge of the design and the other sleeve seam is level. When both sleeves are sewn in turn the sweater inside out, pin the sleeve and side seams from the point under the arm to the edge of the ribbing. Remember to oversew the ribbing.

When sewing seams where the design goes over the shoulder or into the back, use the appropriate colour and yarn instead of the background colour. With a warm iron, press the seams gently.

In each chapter I have talked about the specific problems involved and categorized the pattern as easy, medium-difficult or a Real Brute so that you have some idea of the Nature of the Beast.

Care of Your Beastly Knit

We recommend that because of the Nature of the Beast all these sweaters be dry cleaned.

List of Yarn Suppliers

Jaeger Hand Knitting Ltd
PO Box McMullen Road
Darlington
Co. Durham
DL1 1YQ

Nina A. Miklin
104 Biddulph Mansions
Elgin Avenue
London W9 1HU
Mail Order only
Tel: 01-286 1532

Patricia Roberts Knitting Ltd
31 James Street
London WC2 8PA
Yarns
Tel: 01-379 6660

and at
60 Kinnerton Street
London SW1X 8ES
Mail Order & Yarns
Tel: 01-235 4742

Texere Yarns
College Mill
Barkerend Road
Bradford
W. Yorkshire
BD3 9AQ
Mail Order Only
Tel: 0274 722191

Yarnworks
27 Harcourt Street
London W1
Mail Order
Tel: 01-724 2419

Jaeger Hand Knitting Ltd, Yarnworks and Patricia Roberts Knitting Ltd can be found in various shops and outlets throughout the UK.
Texere Yarns and Nina A. Miklin are both mail order only.

JIMA CAT

I've got this cat called Jima. It should have been possible for you to see for yourselves why I chose to do this particular design, since Jima was supposed to be a cover girl for the day and pose helpfully with me in the photograph. She behaved so badly, and was so difficult, that I'm afraid we gave up and opted for this fabulous fairground cat from my mother's private collection to act as my co-model. Jima was packed off in disgrace, so I shall have to make do with describing her: she is half Abyssinian and half Blue Burmese, and 'Jima' is a town in Abyssinia that my father knows from his travels as a war correspondent for the BBC. Everyone thinks she is called 'Gemma' because her name is pronounced the same but with an 'i', while newspapers whenever they write about me invariably say that I've got a cat called 'Jim', which drives me mad.

Jima comes from a cat breeder in Barking in East London, a somewhat inappropriate place to buy a cat, and she must have been a parrot in a previous existence because she is obsessed with sitting on my shoulder or draping herself around my neck, especially when I'm drawing. She is fascinated by all the little squares and lines on the graph patterns, and watches for as long as I'll let her before the crick in my neck forces me to oust her from her perch.

So, of course, I told my photographer what a funny little creature she was and, needless to say, she decided to lose completely her sense of humour. Perhaps she was jealous of my shoulder being taken over by her knitted equivalent and, although I'm very sorry not to be able to show off the feline inspiration for the Jima Cat Sweater, it is a lot more comfortable wearing the angora-knitted variation on the theme.

This is one of the medium sweaters to knit: for embroidery, see The Nature of the Beast chapter.

15

INSTRUCTIONS: JIMA CAT

MATERIALS
11x25g Nina Miklin Ciocca cotton in Pink
1 reel Nina Miklin fine lurex in Silver
1x20g each of Patricia Roberts angora in Light Grey (Perl), Dark Grey (Acier) and White
1 reel Patricia Roberts Silver lurex
One pair each 2¼mm (No.0) and 3¼mm (No.3) knitting needles
One row counter
One stitch holder
One crochet hook

TENSION
26 stitches and 34 rows to 10cm x 10cm (4in) on size 3¼mm (No.3) needles in St.st. It is important that your tension sample measures exactly the above dimensions to ensure size of sweater. If you have less stitches use a smaller needle, if more stitches then use a larger needle.

MEASUREMENTS
Chest   107cm (42in)
Length   63cm (25in)
Sleeve seam   53cm (21in)

COLOUR CODING
The following instructions refer to the colours as shown here:
A Pink (background)
B Light Grey (with fine lurex)
C Dark Grey
D Light Grey
E White
F Silver lurex (Patricia Roberts)

PREPARATION
Wind off a small amount of Light Grey angora, and divide the remainder into two balls. Pre-wind these with the fine Silver lurex. Divide the White angora into two balls, the Dark Grey into two balls, and wind off a length of thick Silver lurex.

ABBREVIATIONS
K	knit.
P	purl.
st.	stitch.
sts	stitches.
St.st.	Stocking stitch, (one row knit, one row purl alternately).
inc.	increase by working into same stitch twice.
dec.	decrease by working 2 stitches together.
K2tog.	knit 2 stitches together.
P2tog.	purl 2 stitches together.
PU1	pick up the loop between the needles and place on left needle. Work this loop as an extra stitch.

FRONT
With colour A and 2¼mm (No.0) needles cast on 130sts. In single rib (K1, P1) work 30 rows.
Changing to 3¼mm (No.3) needles, and working in St.st., increase one st. at both ends of the first row, the 7th row, the 14th row and every following 7th row until Row 63 (150sts).
Row 64–70: Work in St.st. Turn row counter to 0.

Start Pattern
Row 1: K52A, K4E, K94A.
Row 2: P94A, P7E, P49A.
Row 3: K49A, K10E, K91A.
Row 4: P91A, P10E, P49A.
Row 5: K49A, K10E, K91A.

These five rows set the position of the pattern. Now follow the graph from here to Row 92.
Adjust row counter to Row 172.

Shape Neck
Row 173: Continuing to follow the graph as set, K61, K2tog. Slip next 24sts on to the stitch holder. Join new colour A and K2tog. K61.
Row 174: P60, P2tog. On other side of neck, P2tog. P60.
Repeat these two rows, decreasing one st. at both sides of neck edge, on the next 12 rows (49sts on either side).
Row 187–198: Continue in St.st. and following graph as set.

Shape Shoulders
Continuing to follow graph as set.
Row 199: Cast off 19sts. K30. K other side of neck.
Row 200: Cast off 19sts. P30. P other side of neck.
Row 201: Cast off 15sts. K15. K other side of neck.
Row 202: Cast off 15sts. P15. P other side of neck.
Row 203: Cast off 15sts. K other side of neck.
Row 204: Cast off remaining 15sts.

FRONT NECK BAND
With colour A, 2¼mm (No.0) needles and right side facing, pick up and knit from top left-hand side of neck, 32sts. In single rib (K1, P1) work the 24sts from stitch holder. Then pick up and knit 32sts from the right side of neck. Work in single rib for a further 7 rows.
Cast off loosely in rib.

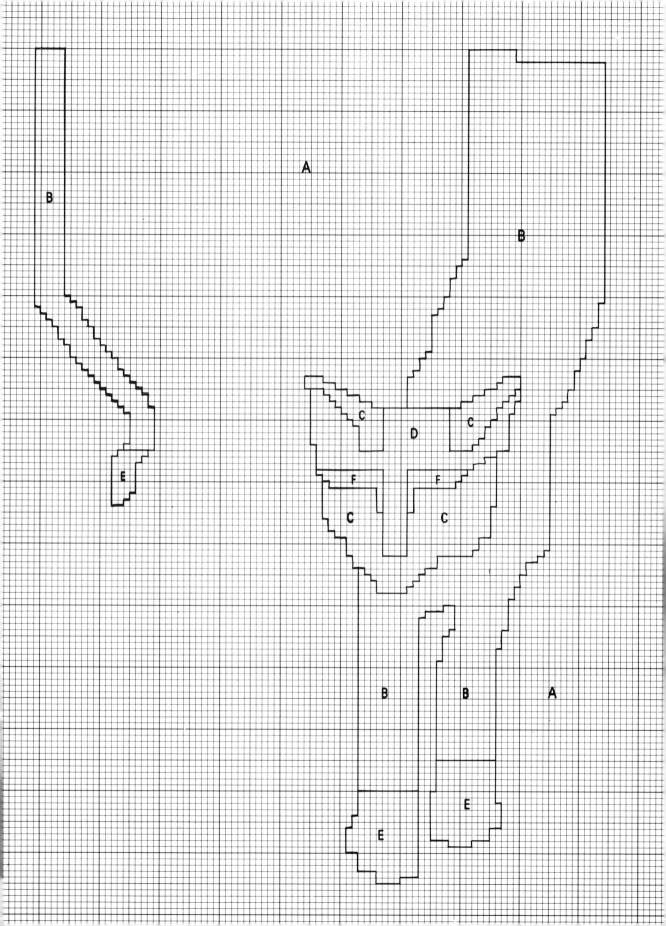

BACK

With colour A and 2¼mm (No. 0) needles cast on 130sts. In single rib (K1, P1) work 30 rows.

Changing to 3¼mm (No. 3) needles, and working in St. st., increase one st. at both ends of the first row, the 7th row, the 14th row and every following 7th row until Row 63 (150sts).

Row 64–98: Work in St. st. Turn row counter to 0.

Start Pattern

Row 1: K110A, K7E, K33A.
Row 2: P31A, P9E, P110A.
Row 3: K109A, K11E, K30A.
Row 4: P30A, P11E, P16A, P5E, P88A.
Row 5: K86A, K4E, K2F, K2E, K14A, K12E, K30A.

These five rows set the position of the pattern. Now follow the graph from here to Row 100.

Adjust row counter to Row 198.

Shape Shoulders

Continuing to follow graph as set:
Row 199: Cast off 19sts. K to end of row.
Row 200: Cast off 19sts. P to end of row.
Row 201: Cast off 15sts. K to end of row.
Row 202: Cast off 15sts. P to end of row.
Row 203: Cast off 15sts. K to end of row.
Row 204: Cast off 15sts. P to end of row.

BACK NECK BAND

Changing to 2¼mm (No. 0) needles, work 8 rows single rib on remaining 52sts. Cast off loosely in rib.

SLEEVES (both alike)

With colour A and 2¼mm (No. 0) needles cast on 66sts. In single rib work 30 rows. Changing to 3¼mm (No. 3) needles, and working in St. st., increase one st. at both ends of the first row, the 3rd row, the 6th row, the 9th row and every following 3rd row until Row 140 (160sts). Cast off loosely.

EMBROIDERY

Refer to the chapter headed The Nature of the Beast, and embroider both eyes and the nose.

MAKING UP

Using the crochet hook, work the loose ends of the yarn through the back of several sts of their own colour, to secure. Do not make knots.

On a flat surface, carefully pin out to size and press each piece.

Do not press the ribbing or the angora.

Sew together the shoulder seams. Find the centre of each sleeve top and line up with shoulder seam. Pin into place and sew, ensuring both armhole side seams are of equal length. Pin side and sleeve seams together and sew.

Press seams gently.

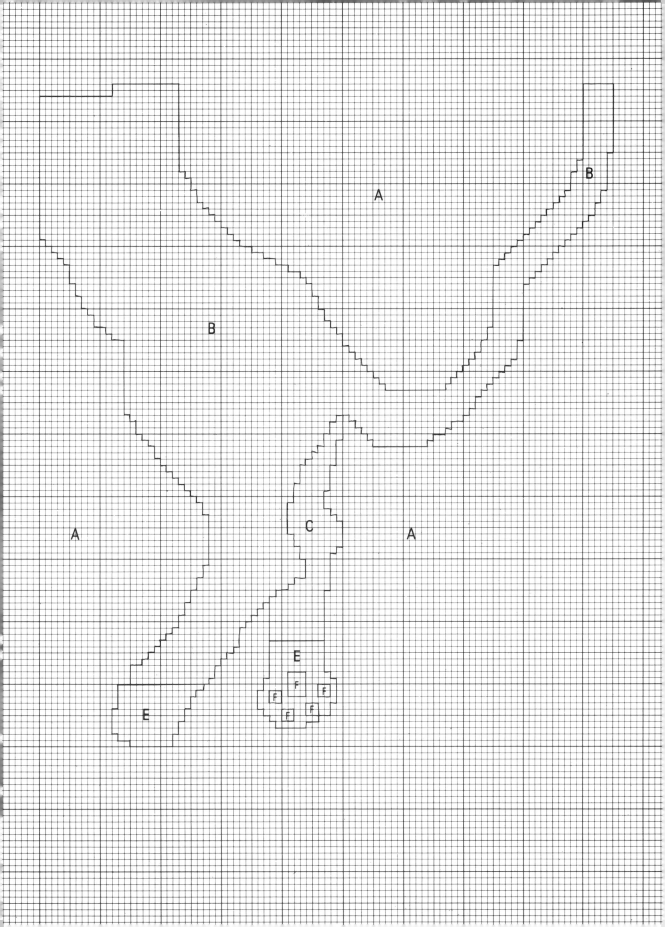

PANDA

When my brother and I were little, our parents used to take us to the London Zoo every day. These visits have proved one of the big influences in my career as an illustrator, and one of my chief sources of inspiration for the animals in this book. One of the superstars of the Zoo in those days was Chi Chi the giant panda. I think it would be impossible not to be fascinated by these extraordinary creatures, and out of the question to do a collection of Beastly Knits without including a Beastly Panda.

I particularly chose the silk and cotton slub which we used for the background for its bamboo-like quality. I know it isn't really at all like bamboo, but it does give a Chinese flavour to the design, don't you think? The animal would look good on almost any brightly coloured background, should you want to go for something less subtle. I think it would be especially effective on a bright red, or green of the sort we used for the Koala Bears.

The Panda is one of the simpler sweaters to knit, very comfortable and easy to wear according to Sally Simpson who is modelling it with such panache. She is accompanied by a fairground zebra; the next best black and white animal in the absence of a fairground panda. Feel relieved that it is only a panda you have to worry about knitting, and that I'm not involving you in getting to grips with all those stripes!

The embroidery is very simple – two circles of tiny chain stitch for the eyes, with a single white stitch in each for the highlights.

22

INSTRUCTIONS: PANDA

MATERIALS
6x50g Yarnworks silk/cotton mix in Brown (Taupe No. 407) 1x20g each of Jaeger angora in White (No. 550) and Black (No. 561)
One pair each 2¼mm (No. 0) and 3mm (No. 2) knitting needles
One row counter
One stitch holder
One crochet hook

TENSION
24 stitches and 30 rows to 10cm x 10cm (4in) on size 3mm (No. 2) needles in St. st. It is important that your tension sample measures exactly the above dimensions to ensure size of sweater. If you have less stitches use a smaller needle, if more then use a larger needle.

MEASUREMENTS
Chest   107cm (42in)
Length   58cm (23in)
Sleeve seam   41cm (16in)

COLOUR CODING
The following instructions refer to the colours as shown here:
A Brown (background)
B White
C Black

PREPARATION
Divide the White into three separate balls and the Black into four balls, with several lengths of Black yarn for nose, ears, etc.

ABBREVIATIONS
K   knit.
P   purl.
st.   stitch.
sts   stitches.
St.st. Stocking stitch, (one row knit, one row purl alternately).
inc.   increase one stitch by working same stitch twice.
dec.   decrease by working 2 stitches together.
K2tog. knit 2 stitches together.
P2tog. purl 2 stitches together.

FRONT
With colour A and 3mm (No. 2) needles cast on 130sts. Work 20 rows in St. st. starting with a K row.
Row 21: As you knit each st. pick up one st. at the back of the needle from the cast-on row, thus making a hem.
Row 22–50: Work in St. st. starting with a P row.
Turn row counter to 0.

Start Pattern
Row 1: K30A, K15C, K35A, K10C, K40A.
Row 2: P40A, P11C, P34A, P16C, P29A.
Row 3: K28A, K17C, K33A, K12C, K40A.
Row 4: P40A, P13C, P32A, P18C, P27A.
Row 5: K26A, K19C, K31A, K14C, K40A.

These five rows set the position of the pattern. Now follow the graph from here to Row 95.
Adjust row counter to Row 145.
Row 146–156: Work in St. st.

Shape Neck
Row 157: K51, K2tog. Slip next 24sts on to the stitch holder. Join new colour A and K2tog. K51.
Row 158: P50, P2tog. On other side of neck, P2tog. P50.
Repeat these two rows,

decreasing one st. at both sides of neck edge, on the next 12 rows (39sts either side of neck).
Row 171–180: Work in St. st. on either side of neck.

Shape Shoulders
Row 181: Cast off 10sts. K29. K other side of neck.
Row 182: Cast off 10sts. P29. P other side of neck.
Row 183: Cast off 10sts. K19. K other side of neck.
Row 184: Cast off 10sts. P19. P other side of neck.
Row 185: Cast off 10sts. K9. K other side of neck.
Row 186: Cast off 10sts. P9. P other side of neck.
Row 187: Cast off 9sts. K other side of neck.
Row 188: Cast off remaining 9sts.

FRONT NECK BAND
With colour A, 2¼mm (No. 0) needles and right side facing, pick up and knit from top left-hand side of neck, 32sts. In single rib (K1, P1) work the 24sts from stitch holder. Then pick up and knit 32sts from the right side of neck. Work in single rib for a further 7 rows.
Cast off loosely in rib.

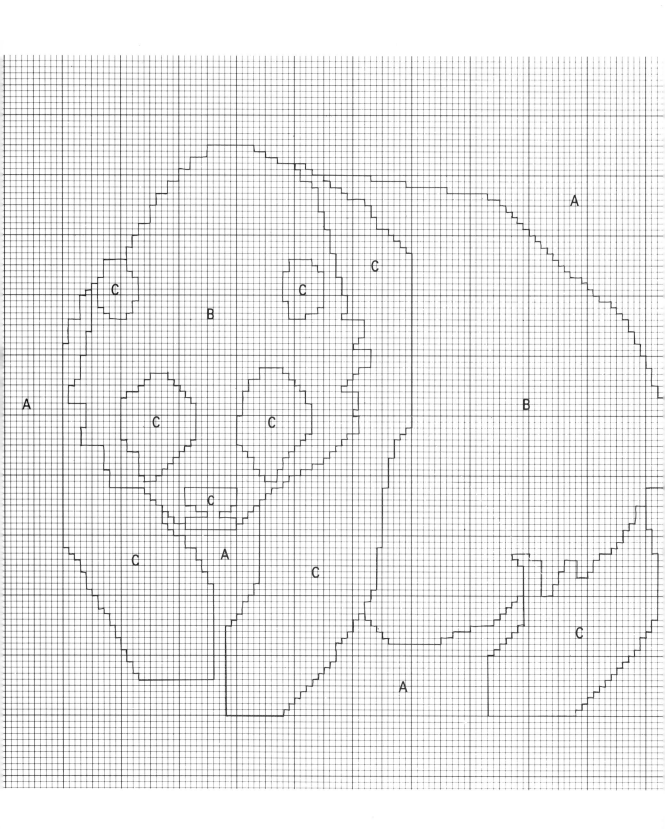

BACK

With colour A and 3mm
(No.2) needles cast on
130sts.
Row 1–21: Work exactly as
for Front.
Row 22–180: Work in St. st.

Shape Shoulders

Row 181: Cast off 10sts. K to
end of row.
Row 182: Cast off 10sts. P to
end of row.
Row 183: Cast off 10sts. K to
end of row.
Row 184: Cast off 10sts. P to
end of row.
Row 185: Cast off 10sts. K to
end of row.
Row 186: Cast off 10sts. P to
end of row.
Row 187: Cast off 9sts. K to
end of row.
Row 188: Cast off 9sts. P to
end of row.

BACK NECK BAND

Changing to 2¼mm (No.0)
needles, work 8 rows single
rib on remaining 52sts.
Cast off loosely in rib.

SLEEVES (both alike)

With colour A and 3mm
(No.2) needles cast on
110sts. Work 20 rows in
St. st. starting with a K row.
Row 21: As you knit each st.
pick up one st. at the back of
the needle from the cast-on
row, thus making a hem.
Row 22–130: Work in St. st.
Cast off loosely.

EMBROIDERY

Refer to the chapter headed
The Nature of the Beast, and
embroider the eyes.

MAKING UP

Using the crochet hook,
work the loose ends of the
yarn through the back of
several sts of their own
colour, to secure. Do not
make knots.
On a flat surface, carefully pin
out to size and press each
piece.
Do not press the ribbing.
Sew together the shoulder
seams. Find the centre of
each sleeve top and line up
with shoulder seam. Pin into
place and sew, ensuring both
armhole side seams are of
equal length. Pin side and
sleeve seams together and
sew.
Press seams gently.

SADDLEBACK PIG & PIGLETS

I've always loved drawing animals, but I don't think I had ever drawn a pig until I met Lord and Lady Birkett, and the Honourable Thomas Piglett. I know that quite a few people collect pigs these days, but I don't believe anyone has more in the way of pig paraphernalia than the Birketts. So, in order to keep up with their porkishness, I had to learn how to draw pig cards, paint pig pictures for Thomas, make pig mugs and pots, and embroider pig cushions. I can manage Danish Landrace Hogs, Gloucester Old Spots, Tamworth Sows, British Saddlebacks, Warthogs, Bearded Pigs, Wild Boar and Giant Forest Hogs. I'm a Pig Expert. So Beastly Knits would simply not have been the same without a pig sweater or two, and no one else but Gloria and Thomas would have been right to model them for me. We made the somewhat stylized Saddlebacks big enough for a man, but Gloria, like me, loves huge baggy sweaters and was perfectly happy wearing this one. Thomas, who is three, had a great time riding the little fairground porker, and an even better time playing with the camera and being shown by Colin how to work the flash and all that sort of technical stuff.

You will find both of these sweaters easy to knit, except for their tails which are a bit piggy, and the embroidery is easy. I've used fine gold thread to make the rings in their noses – you could give the Piglets nose-rings, too, if you felt like it. See the chapter headed The Nature of the Beast.

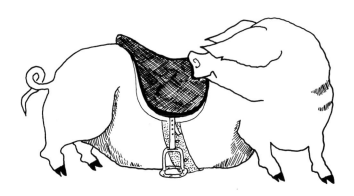

Instructions: Saddleback Pig

MATERIALS

20x25g Patricia Roberts fine cotton in Blue (No. 4)
1x25g Patricia Roberts fine cotton in Black (No. 8)
1x25g each of Nina Miklin Vogue wool in Dark Brown (No. 936) and Beige (No. 934) One pair each 2¼mm (No. 0) and 2¾mm (No. 1) knitting needles
One row counter
One stitch holder
One crochet hook

TENSION

32 stitches and 38 rows to 10cm x 10cm (4in) on size 2¾mm (No. 1) needles in St. st. It is important that your tension sample measures exactly the above dimensions to ensure size of sweater. If you have less stitches use a smaller needle, if more use a larger needle.

MEASUREMENTS

Chest   109cm (43in)
Length   66cm (26in)
Sleeve seam   61cm (24in)

COLOUR CODING

The following instructions refer to the colours as shown here:
A Blue (background)
B Dark Brown
C Beige
D Black

PREPARATION

Divide the Dark Brown into two large and one small ball, the Black into four small balls.

ABBREVIATIONS

K	knit.
P	purl.
st.	stitch.
sts	stitches.
St. st.	Stocking stitch, (one row knit, one row purl alternately).
inc.	increase by working into same stitch twice.
dec.	decrease by working 2 stitches together.
K2tog.	knit 2 stitches together.
P2tog.	purl 2 stitches together.

FRONT

With colour A and 2¼mm (No. 0) needles cast on 140sts. In single rib (K1, P1) work 30 rows.
Changing to 2¾mm (No. 1) needles, and working in St. st., increase one st. at both ends of the first row, the 7th row, the 14th row and every following 7th row until Row 63 (160sts).
Row 64–80: Work in St. st.
Turn row counter to 0.

Start Pattern

Row 1: K43A, K2D, K4A, K2D, K54A, K2D, K7A, K2D, K44A.
Row 2: P44A, P2D, P7A, P2D, P54A, P2D, P4A, P2D, P43A.
Row 3: K43A, K2D, K4A, K3D, K52A, K4D, K3A, K5D, K44A.
Row 4: P44A, P7D, P1A, P5D, P51A, P4D, P3A, P3D, P42A.
Row 5: K42A, K3D, K2A, K6D, K50A, K5D, K1A, K7D, K44A.

These five rows set the position of the pattern. Now follow the graph from here to Row 108.
Adjust row counter to Row 188.
Row 189–200: Work in St. st.

Shape Neck

Row 201: K65, K2tog. Slip next 26sts on to the stitch holder. Join new colour A and K2tog. K65.
Row 202: P64, P2tog. On other side of neck P2tog. P64.
Repeat these two rows, decreasing one st. at both sides of neck edge, on the next 12 rows (53sts on either side).
Row 215–226: Work in St. st. on both sides of neck.

Shape Shoulders

Row 227: Cast off 13sts. K40. K other side of neck.
Row 228: Cast off 13sts. P40. P other side of neck.
Row 229: Cast off 13sts. K27. K other side of neck.
Row 230: Cast off 13sts. P27. P other side of neck.
Row 231: Cast off 13sts. K14. K other side of neck.
Row 232: Cast off 13sts. P14. P other side of neck.
Row 233: Cast off 14sts. K other side of neck.
Row 234: Cast off remaining 14sts.

FRONT NECK BAND

With colour A, 2¼mm (No. 0) needles and right side facing, pick up and knit from top left-hand side of neck, 34sts. In single rib (K1, P1) work the 26sts from stitch holder. Then pick up and knit 34sts from the right side of neck. Work in single rib for a further 7 rows.
Cast off loosely in rib.

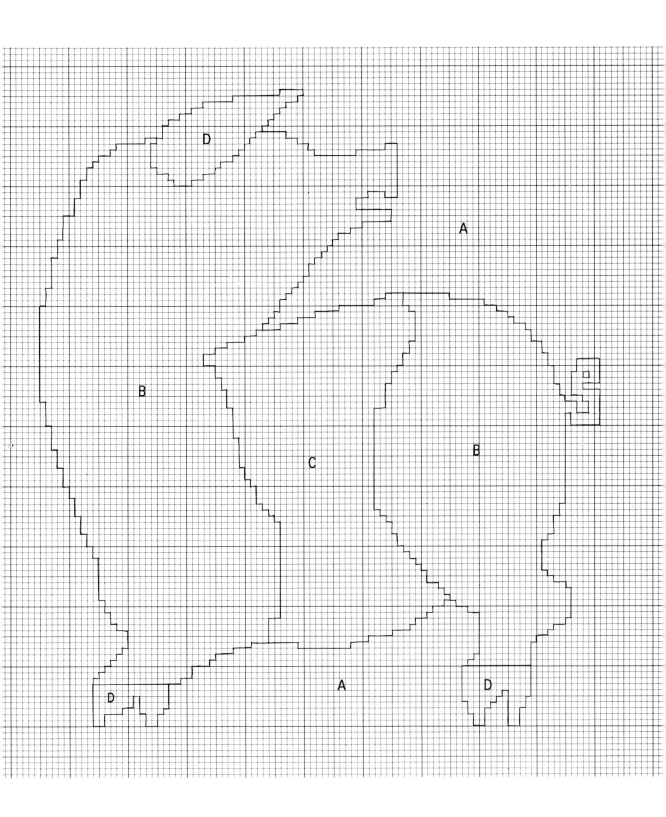

BACK

With colour A and 2¼mm (No.0) needles cast on 140sts. In single rib (K1,P1) work 30 rows.
Changing to 2¾mm (No.1) needles, and working in St.st., increase one st. at both ends of the first row, the 7th row, the 14th row and every following 7th row until Row 63 (160sts).
Row 64–80: Work in St.st. starting with a P row.
Turn row counter to 0.

Start Pattern

Row 1: K33A, K2D, K4A, K2D, K54A, K2D, K7A, K2D, K54A.
Row 2: P54A, P2D, P7A, P2D, P54A, P2D, P4A, P2D, P33A.
Row 3: K33A, K2D, K4A, K3D, K52A, K4D, K3A, K5D, K54A.
Row 4: P54A, P7D, P1A, P5D, P51A, P4D, P3A, P3D, P32A.
Row 5: K32A, K3D, K2A, K6D, K50A, K5D, K1A, K7D, K54A.

These five rows set the position of the pattern. Now follow the graph from here to Row 72.
Adjust row counter to Row 152.
Row 153–226: Work in St.st.

Shape Shoulders

Row 227: Cast off 13sts. K to end of row.
Row 228: Cast off 13sts. P to end of row.
Row 229: Cast off 13sts. K to end of row.
Row 230: Cast off 13sts. P to end of row.
Row 231: Cast off 13sts. K to end of row.
Row 232: Cast off 13sts. P to end of row.
Row 233: Cast off 14sts. K to end of row.
Row 234: Cast off 14sts. P to end of row.

BACK NECK BAND

Changing to 2¼mm (No.0) needles, work 8 rows single rib on remaining 54sts.
Cast off loosely in rib.

SLEEVES (both alike)

With colour A and 2¼mm (No.0) needles cast on 70sts. In single rib work 30 rows.
Changing to 2¾mm (No.1) needles, and working in St.st., increase one st. at both ends of the first row, the 4th row, the 8th row and every following 4th row until Row 176 (160sts). Work a further 4 rows.
Cast off loosely.

EMBROIDERY

Refer to the chapter headed The Nature of the Beast, and embroider the eyes and a ring in the nose.

MAKING UP

Using the crochet hook, work the loose ends of the yarn through the back of several sts of their own colour, to secure. Do not make knots.
On a flat surface, carefully pin out to size and press each piece.
Do not press the ribbing.
Sew together the shoulder seams. Find the centre of each sleeve top and line up with shoulder seam. Pin into place and sew, ensuring both armhole side seams are of equal length. Pin side and sleeve seams together and sew.
Press seams gently.

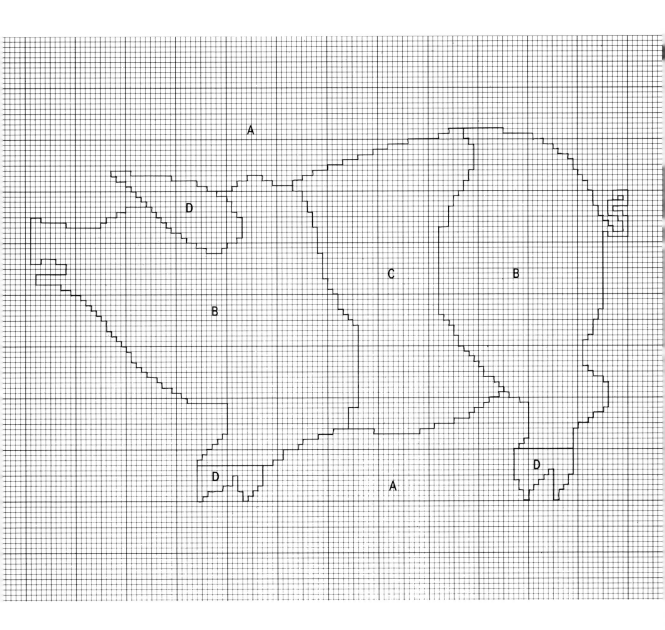

INSTRUCTIONS: PIGLETS

MATERIALS
3x50g Jaeger alpaca in Light Grey (Paloma No.148)
2x25g Patricia Roberts fine cotton in Pink (No.19)
1x25g Patricia Roberts fine cotton in Black (No.8)
One pair each 2¼mm (No.0) and 3mm (No.2) knitting needles
One row counter
One stitch holder
One crochet hook

TENSION
26 stitches and 34 rows to 10cm x 10cm (4in) on size 3mm (No.2) needles in St.st. It is important that your tension sample measures exactly the above dimensions to ensure size of sweater. If you have less stitches use a smaller needle, if more stitches use a larger needle.

MEASUREMENTS
Chest   81cm (32in)
Length   35cm (14in)
Sleeve seam 30cm (12in)

COLOUR CODING
The following instructions refer to the colours as shown here:
A Light Grey (background)
B Pink
C Black

PREPARATION
Divide the Pink into two balls each, the Black in four very small balls.

ABBREVIATIONS
K   knit.
P   purl.
st.   stitch.
sts   stitches.
St.st. Stocking stitch, (one row knit, one row purl alternately).
inc.   increase one stitch by working same stitch twice.
dec.   decrease by working 2 stitches together.
K2tog. knit 2 stitches together.
P2tog. purl 2 stitches together.

FRONT
With colour A and 2¼mm (No.0) needles cast on 110sts. In single rib (K1,P1) work 25 rows.
Changing to 3mm (No.2) needles, work 10 rows in St.st. starting with a K row. Turn row counter to 0.

Start Pattern
Row 1: K27A, K1C, K61A, K1C K20A.
Row 2: P18A, P3C, P56A, P1C, P4A, P2C, P26A.
Row 3: K25A, K3C, K3A, K2C, K56A, K4C, K17A.
Row 4: P16A, P5C, P3A, P3C, P50A, P3C, P2A, P4C, P24A.
Row 5: K23A, K5C, K1A, K4C, K50A, K4C, K2A, K6C, K15A.

These five rows set the position of the pattern. Now follow the graph from here to Row 62.
Adjust row counter to Row 72.
Row 73–100: Work in St.st.

Shape Neck
Row 101: K43, K2tog. Slip next 20sts on to the stitch holder. Join new colour A and K2tog. K43.
Row 102: P42, P2tog. On other side of neck P2tog. P42.
Repeat these two rows, decreasing one st. at both sides of neck edge, on the next 8 rows (35sts on either side).
Row 111–118: Work in St.st. on both sides of neck.

Shape Shoulders
Row 119: Cast off 12sts. K23. K other side of neck.
Row 120: Cast off 12sts. P23. P other side of neck.
Row 121: Cast off 12sts. K11. K other side of neck.
Row 122: Cast off 12sts. P11. P other side of neck.
Row 123: Cast off 11sts. K other side of neck.
Row 124: Cast off remaining 11sts.

FRONT NECK BAND
With colour A, 2¼mm (No.0) needles and right side facing, pick up and knit from top left-hand side of neck, 24sts. In single rib (K1,P1) work the 20sts from stitch holder. Then pick up and knit 24sts from the right side of neck. Work in single rib for a further 7 rows.
Cast off loosely in rib.

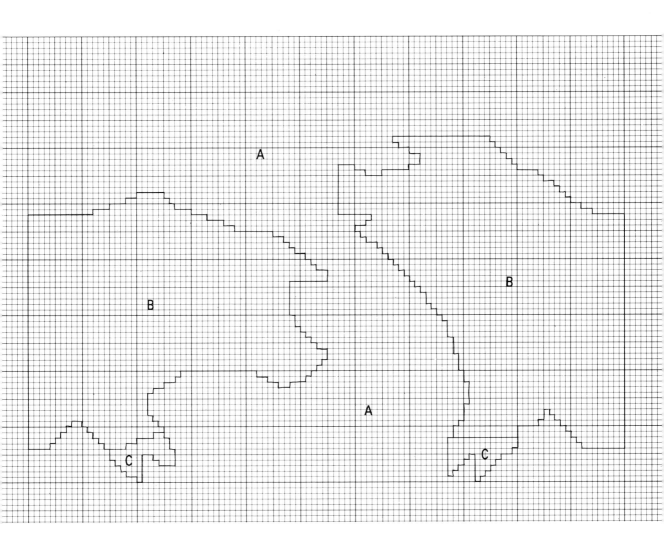

A

B

B

A

C

C

35

BACK

With colour A and 2¼mm (No.0) needles cast on 110sts. In single rib (K1,P1) work 25 rows.
Changing to 3mm (No.2) needles, work 10 rows in St.st. starting with a K row.
Turn row counter to 0.

Start Pattern

Row 1: K20A, K2C, K3A, K2C, K56A, K2C, K3A, K2C, K20A.
Row 2: P20A, P3C, P2A, P2C, P56A, P2C, P2A, P3C, P20A.
Row 3: K20A, K4C, K1A, K3C, K54A, K3C, K1A, K4C, K20A.
Row 4: P20A, P9C, P52A, P9C, P20A.
Row 5: K20A, K9C, K52A, K9C, K20A.

These five rows set the position of the pattern. Now follow the graph from here to Row 53.
Adjust row counter to Row 63.
Row 64–118: Work in St.st.

Shape Shoulders

Row 119: Cast off 12sts. K to end of row.
Row 120: Cast off 12sts. P to end of row.
Row 121: Cast off 12sts. K to end of row.
Row 122: Cast off 12sts. P to end of row.
Row 123: Cast off 11sts. K to end of row.
Row 124: Cast off 11sts. P to end of row.

BACK NECK BAND

Changing to 2¼mm (No.0) needles, work 8 rows single rib on remaining 40sts.
Cast off loosely in rib.

SLEEVES (both alike)

With colour A and 2¼mm (No.0) needles cast on 60sts.
In single rib (K1,P1) work 25 rows.
Changing to 3mm (No.2) needles, and working in St.st., increase one st. at both ends of the first row, the 4th row, the 8th row and every following 4th row until Row 86 (100sts).
Work 4 more rows St.st.
Cast off loosely.

EMBROIDERY

Refer to the chapter headed The Nature of the Beast, and embroider two eyes.

MAKING UP

Using the crochet hook, work the loose ends of the yarn through the back of several sts of their own colour, to secure. Do not make knots.
On a flat surface, carefully pin out to size and press each piece.
Do not press the ribbing.
Pin and sew together the shoulder seams. Find the centre of each sleeve top, line up with shoulder seam. Pin into place and sew, ensuring both armhole side seams are of equal length.
Pin side and sleeve seams together and sew.
Press seams gently.

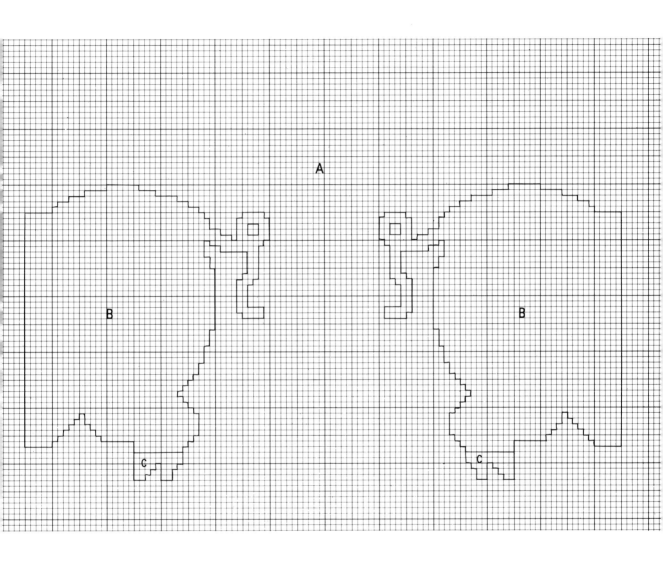

A

B

B

C

C

37

BAT

My friend Andrew Logan is a brilliant sculptor, makes the most beautiful jewellery, is altogether amazing, and didn't bat an eyelid at the thought of wearing this bizarre sweater. Watch out, Vincent Price! I suspect Andrew rather enjoyed himself doing horror-movie acting for the photograph.

I originally designed the sweater to be worn by women rather than men, mainly because Colin Thomas, my photographer, and I decided that it would be good fun to have someone hanging upside down for the photograph, and I could not think of anyone else, besides myself, who would be silly enough to agree to such antics. Andrew Logan, however, doesn't need to hang upside down to look dramatic so, thank heavens, I was saved!

I'm not suggesting that if you were to knit this for a woman, she would have to hang from the rafters to look good in it, though, in fact, it was rather a daft idea all round since the bat would have been the right way up if . . . oh dear! The pattern is just about as complicated as my justifications for the photograph, but do try. It's worth it. The wings are hard to get off the ground, and you might find yourself driven into the belfry with the fine lurex we used for the body. I've added it to give a bit more glitter and glamour to the sweater, but this is entirely up to you, and do by all means leave out the lurex if you think you will go completely batty trying to cope with it. Console yourself, anyway, with the fact that the embroidery is negligible – one French knot for the bat's eye, never mind whether he can bat the lid or not.

INSTRUCTIONS: BAT

MATERIALS
19x20g Texere Yarns 50/50 silk/wool mix in Red (No. 1836)
4x20g Texere Yarns 50/50 silk/wool in Black (No. 1813)
1x25g Patricia Roberts fine cotton in Charcoal Grey
1 reel Nina Miklin fine lurex in Bronze (optional)
One pair each 2¾mm (No.1) and 3¼mm (No.3) knitting needles
One row counter
One stitch holder
One crochet hook

TENSION
26 stitches and 33 rows to 10cm x 10cm (4in) on size 3¼mm (No.3) needles in St.st. It is important that your tension sample measures exactly the above dimensions to ensure size of sweater. If you have less stitches use a smaller needle, if more stitches then use a larger needle.

MEASUREMENTS
Chest   101cm (40in)
Length   53cm (21in)
Sleeve seam 63cm (25in)

COLOUR CODING
The following instructions refer to the colours as shown here:
A Red (background)
B Black
C Charcoal Grey
D Charcoal Grey with Bronze lurex (optional)
NB: If lurex is not used then Code D becomes C.

PREPARATION
Divide the Charcoal Grey into about four separate balls, and if using lurex, wind one together with the lurex.

ABBREVIATIONS
K   knit.
P   purl.
st.   stitch.
sts   stitches.
St.st.   Stocking stitch, (one row knit, one row purl alternately).
inc.   increase one stitch by working twice into same stitch.
dec.   decrease by working 2 stitches together.
K2tog.   knit 2 stitches together.
P2tog.   purl 2 stitches together.
PU1   pick up the loop between the needles and place on left needle. Work this loop as an extra stitch.

FRONT
With colour A and 2¾mm (No.1) needles cast on 120sts. In single rib (K1,P1) work 30 rows.
Changing to 3¼mm (No.3) needles K10, PU1, K10, PU1. Repeat to end of row, ending with K10 (130sts).
Row 2–50: Work in St.st. starting with a P row.
Turn row counter to 0.

Start Pattern
Row 1: K72A, K4C, K54A.
Row 2: P54A, P5C, P71A.
Row 3: K57A, K4C, K8A, K8C, K53A.
Row 4: P6C, P47A, P9C, P6A, P7C, P43A, P4B, P8C.
Row 5: K8C, K6B, K38A, K11C, K4A, K10C, K44A, K3B, K6C.

These five rows set the position of the pattern. Now follow the graph from here to Row 83.
Adjust row counter to Row 133.

Shape Neck
Row 134: P51, P2tog. Slip next 24sts on to the stitch holder. Join new colour A and P2tog. P51.
Row 135: K50, K2tog. On other side of neck, K2tog. K50.
Repeat these two rows, decreasing one st. at both sides of neck edge, on the next 8 rows (43sts on either side).
Row 144–157: Work in St.st. on both sides of neck.

Shape Shoulders
Row 158: Cast off 14sts. P29. P other side of neck.
Row 159: Cast off 14sts. K29. K other side of neck.
Row 160: Cast off 14sts. P15. P other side of neck.
Row 161: Cast off 14sts. K15. K other side of neck.
Row 165: Cast off 15sts. K other side of neck.
Row 166: Cast off remaining 15sts.

FRONT NECK BAND
With colour A, 2¾mm (No.1) needles and right side facing, pick up and knit from top left-hand side of neck, 30sts. In single rib (K1,P1) work the 24sts from stitch holder. Then pick up and knit 30sts from the right side of neck. Work in single rib for a further 7 rows.
Cast off loosely in rib.

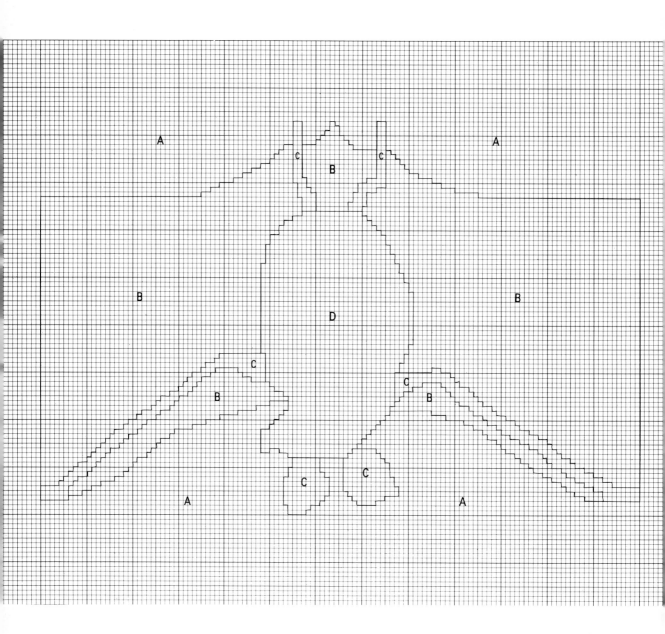

BACK

With colour A and 2¾mm (No.1) needles cast on 120sts. In single rib (K1, P1) work 30 rows.
Changing to 3¼mm (No.3) needles, K10, PU1, K10, PU1. Repeat 8 times, K10 (130sts).
Row 2–157: Work in St.st. beginning with a P row.

Shape Shoulders

Row 158: Cast off 14sts. P to end of row.
Row 159: Cast off 14sts. K to end of row.
Row 160: Cast off 14sts. P to end of row.
Row 161: Cast off 14sts. K to end of row.
Row 162: Cast off 15sts. P to end of row.
Row 163: Cast off 15sts. K to end of row.

BACK NECK BAND

Changing to 2¾mm (No.1) needles, work 8 rows single rib (K1, P1) on remaining 44sts.
Cast off loosely in rib.

RIGHT SLEEVE

The sleeves are worked from waist to shoulder and back to waist.
With colour A and 3¼mm (No.3) needles, cast on 10sts.
Row 1: K.
Row 2: P.
Row 3: K10, cast on 6sts.
Row 4: P16.
Row 5: K16, cast on 6sts.
Row 6: P22.
Row 7: K22, cast on 6sts.
Row 8: P28.
Row 9–18: Continue to cast on 6 sts at the end of every K row (58sts).

Row 19: K21A, K3C, K34A, cast on 6sts.
Row 20: P41A, P2C, P21A.
Row 21: K21A, K2C, K41A, cast on 6sts.
Row 22: P45A, P25C.
Row 23: K28C, K42A, cast on 5sts. (75sts).
Row 24–72: Following the graph as set, increase one st. at the end of every K row, and the beginning of every P row.
Row 73–94: Still following the graph as set, increase one st. at the end of each K row (135sts).
Row 95–165: Completing the graph as set, continue in colour A in St.st. (135sts).
Row 166–187: P2tog. at beginning of each P row.
Row 188–235: Decrease one st. at curved seam edge on every row.
Row 236: Cast off 5sts. P70.
Row 237: K70.
Row 238: Cast off 6sts. P64.
Row 239: K64.
Continue to cast off 6sts at beginning of each P row until 10sts. remain. K one row and cast off.

LEFT SLEEVE

With colour A and 3¼mm (No.3) needles, cast on 10sts.
Row 1: K10.
Row 2: P10.
Row 3: Cast on 6sts., K16.
Row 4: P16.
Row 5: Cast on 6sts., K22.
Row 6: P22.
Row 7: Cast on 6sts., K28.
Row 8: P28.
Row 9–18: Continue to cast on 6sts. at beginning of every K row.
Row 19: Cast on 6sts. and K40A, K3C, K21A.

Row 20: P21A, P2C, P41A.
Row 21: Cast on 6sts. and K47A, K2C, K21A.
Row 22: Join colour C and P25, P45A.
Row 23: Cast on 5sts, and K47A, K28C (75sts).
Row 24–72: Following the graph as set, increase one st. at the beginning of every K row and one st. at the end of every P row.
Row 73–94: Still following the graph as set, increase one st. at the beginning of each K row (135sts).
Row 95–165: Completing the graph as set, continue in colour A in St.st. (135sts).
Row 166–187: P2tog. at end of each P row.
Row 188–234: Decrease one st. at curved seam edge on every row.
Row 235: Cast off 5sts. K to end.
Row 236: P70.
Row 237: Cast off 6sts. K to end.
Row 238: P64.
Row 239: Cast off 6sts. K to end.
Continue to cast off 6sts at beginning of each K row until 10sts remain. P one row and cast off.

CUFFS (both alike)

With colour A and 2¾mm (No.1) needles cast on 66sts. and work 15 rows in single rib (K1, P1).
Cast off loosely in rib.

EMBROIDERY

Refer to the chapter headed The Nature of the Beast, and embroider an eye, and both feet on ribbing at neck.

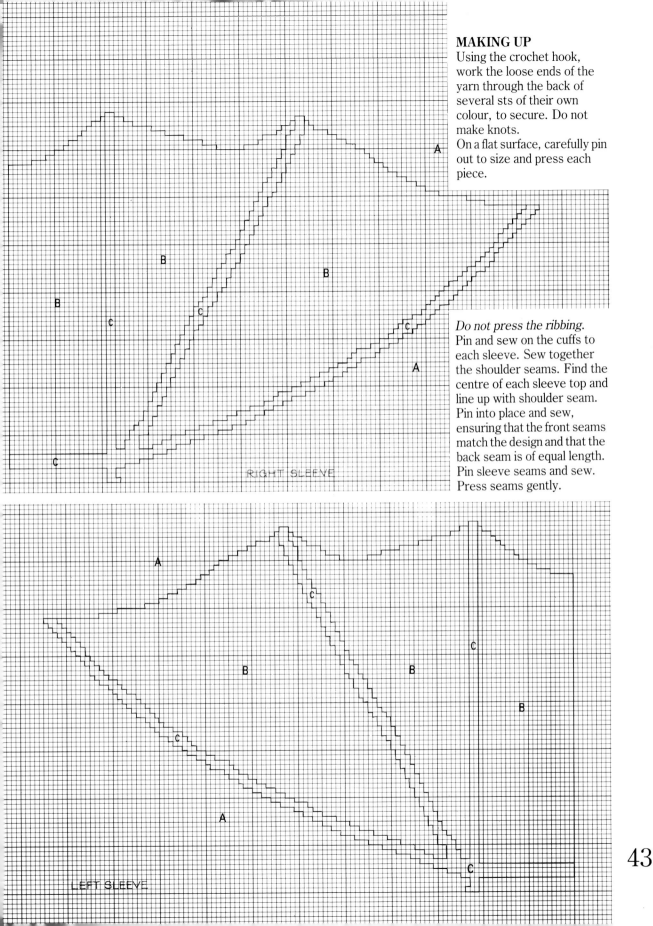

MAKING UP

Using the crochet hook, work the loose ends of the yarn through the back of several sts of their own colour, to secure. Do not make knots.

On a flat surface, carefully pin out to size and press each piece.

Do not press the ribbing. Pin and sew on the cuffs to each sleeve. Sew together the shoulder seams. Find the centre of each sleeve top and line up with shoulder seam. Pin into place and sew, ensuring that the front seams match the design and that the back seam is of equal length. Pin sleeve seams and sew. Press seams gently.

RIGHT SLEEVE

LEFT SLEEVE

43

Cow

Anni Bowes, who is modelling the Cow for me, was responsible for knitting every one of these twenty-nine sweaters in an unbelievably short time with good humour and never-ending patience. I shall be eternally grateful to her for all her help and encouragement.

She chose to wear the Cow because she just happens to collect cows. She decided to collect cows because the market for pig, dog, cat and frog collections seemed to be cornered, with the poor old cow getting left out in the field. She has since discovered that she is not alone, because it is possible to buy every conceivable type of collectable cow except, as far as she can tell, a Cow Sweater. So here, for all of you who want to come out of the cowshed, is the original Beastly Jersey.

I found that by adding the little bits of pink for the cow's nose and udder that the whole pattern was brought to life. It is extraordinary how you can transform a basically dull black and white design by adding just one splash of a different colour. It makes the sweater a little more complicated, but it is worth it. And you could hardly describe it as a Real Brute to knit, just medium-difficult, so try not to get too cheesed off, pour yourself a large glass of milk, forgive me for buttering you up with all these gruesome puns and console yourself with the fact that the embroidery is easy. You only have the eyes to do with the usual circle of black and a white highlight, as explained in The Nature of the Beast chapter.

45

INSTRUCTIONS: COW

MATERIALS

17x20g Texere Yarns 50/50 silk/wool mix in Sage Green (No.1845)
2x20g Texere Yarns 50/50 silk/wool mix in Black (No.1813)
1x20g Texere Yarns 50/50 silk/wool mix in White (No.1824)
1x25g Patricia Roberts fine cotton in Pink (No.19)
One pair each 3mm (No.2) and 3¾mm (No.4) knitting needles
One row counter
One stitch holder
One crochet hook

TENSION

26 stitches and 33 rows to 10cm x 10cm (4in) on size 3¾mm (No.4) needles in St.st. It is important that your tension sample measures exactly the above dimensions to ensure size of sweater. If you have less stitches use a smaller needle, if more stitches then use a larger needle.

MEASUREMENTS

Chest	99cm (39in)
Length	58cm (23in)
Sleeve seam	56cm (22in)

COLOUR CODING

The following instructions refer to the colours as shown here:
A Sage Green (background)
B Black
C White
D Pink

PREPARATION

Divide both Black balls in half, the White into four separate smaller balls, and the Pink into three.

ABBREVIATIONS

K	knit.
P	purl.
st.	stitch.
sts	stitches.
St.st.	Stocking stitch, (one row knit, one row purl alternately).
inc.	increase one stitch by working twice into same stitch.
dec.	decrease by working 2 stitches together.
K2tog.	knit 2 stitches together.
P2tog.	purl 2 stitches together.
PU1	pick up the loop between the needles and place on left needle. Work this loop as an extra stitch.

FRONT

With colour A and 3mm (No.2) needles cast on 120sts. In single rib (K1,P1) work 30 rows.
Changing to 3¾mm (No.4) needles, K10, PU1, K10, PU1, repeat 9 more times, K10 (130sts).
Work 24 rows in St.st. starting with a P row.
Turn row counter to 0̇.

Start Pattern

Row 1: P25A, P8C, P57A, P9C, P31A.
Row 2: K31A, K9C, K57A, K8C, K25A.
Row 3: P25A, P8C, P57A, P8C, P5B, P27A.
Row 4: K27A, K6B, K7C, K58A, K7C, K25A.
Row 5: P25A, P7C, P58A, P7C, P6B, P27A.

These five rows set the position of the pattern. Now

follow the graph from here to Row 109.
Adjust row counter to Row 134.
Row 135–150: Work in St.st.

Shape Neck

Row 151: K51, K2tog. Slip next 24sts on to the stitch holder. Join new colour A and K2tog. K51.
Row 152: P50, P2tog. On other side of neck P2tog. P50.
Repeat these two rows, decreasing one st. at both sides of neck edge, on the next 8 rows (43sts on either side).
Row 161–174: Work in St.st. on both sides of neck.

Shape Shoulders

Row 175: Cast off 14sts. K29. K other side of neck.
Row 176: Cast off 14sts. P29. P other side of neck.
Row 177: Cast off 14sts. K15. K other side of neck.
Row 178: Cast off 14sts. P15. P other side of neck.
Row 179: Cast off 15sts. K other side of neck.
Row 180: Cast off remaining 15sts.

FRONT NECK BAND

With colour A, 3mm (No.2) needles and right side facing, pick up and knit from top left-hand side of neck, 30sts. In single rib (K1,P1) work the 24sts from stitch holder. Then pick up and knit 30sts from the right side of neck. Work in single rib for a further 7 rows.
Cast off loosely in rib.

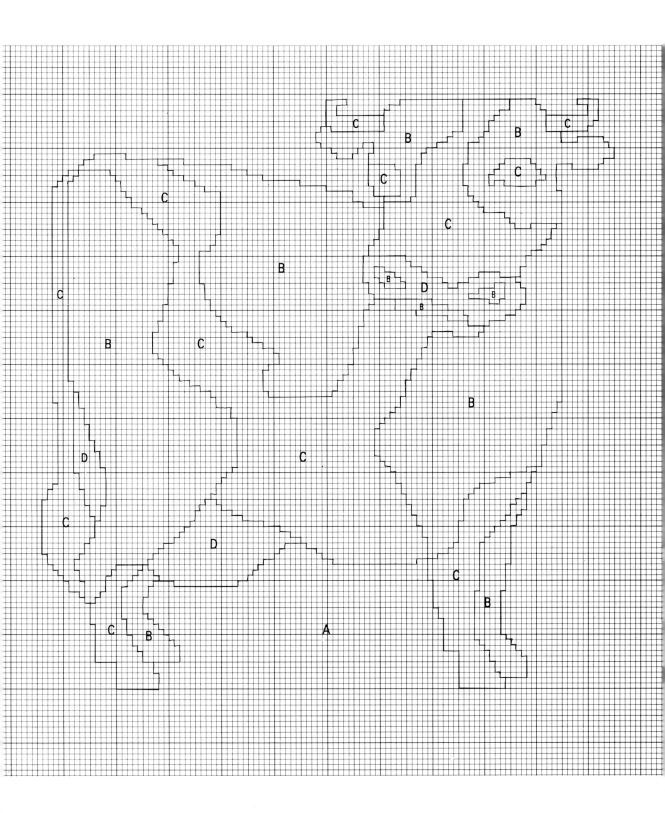

BACK

With colour A and 3mm
(No. 2) needles cast on
120sts. In single rib (K1, P1)
work 30 rows.
Changing to 3¾mm (No. 4)
needles, K10, PU1, K10,
PU1, repeat to end, K10
(130sts).
Row 2–174: Work in St. st.
starting with a P row.

Shape Shoulders

Row 175: Cast off 14sts. K to
end of row.
Row 176: Cast off 14sts. P to
end of row.
Row 177: Cast off 14sts. K to
end of row.
Row 178: Cast off 14sts. P to
end of row.
Row 179: Cast off 15sts. K to
end of row.
Row 180: Cast off 15sts. P to
end of row.

BACK NECK BAND

Changing to 3mm (No. 2)
needles, work 8 rows single
rib on remaining 44sts.
Cast off loosely in rib.

SLEEVES (both alike)

With colour A and 3mm
(No. 2) needles cast on 66sts.
In single rib (K1, P1) work 30
rows.
Changing to 3¾mm (No. 4)
needles, and working in
St. st., increase one st. at
both ends of the first row, the
4th row, the 8th row and
every following 4th row until
Row 130 (132sts).
Cast off loosely.

EMBROIDERY

Refer to the chapter headed
The Nature of the Beast, and
embroider both eyes.

MAKING UP

Using the crochet hook,
work the loose ends of the
yarn through the back of
several sts of their own
colour, to secure. Do not
make knots.
On a flat surface, carefully pin
out to size and press each
piece.
Do not press the ribbing.
Sew together the shoulder
seams. Find the centre of
each sleeve top and line up
with shoulder seam. Pin into
place and sew, ensuring both
armhole side seams are of
equal length. Pin side and
sleeve seams together and
sew.
Press seams gently.

POLAR BEAR
& BABY SEAL

Bruce Fogle, who is wearing the Polar Bear, is, according to my
cats Dart and Jima, the best veterinarian in London, although my
step-cat, Killer, is less enthusiastic following a rather fur-raising
journey to the Portman Veterinary Clinic for his annual 'flu jab.
Bruce comes from Canada, so it seemed appropriate to ask him to
model the Polar Bear Sweater, and I have him to thank for giving
me the idea to do Beastly Knits in the first place. He asked me if I
would design an Old English Sheepdog Sweater for a friend of his
and, having done that, I thought that it would be a good idea to put
together a whole book of different animal designs. So, ultimately,
it is thanks to Dart and Jima for introducing me to Bruce. One day
I'll design a special Killer sweater, so that he doesn't feel left out of
all this, and Dart and Jima won't be quite as smug and pleased with
themselves for having orchestrated the whole enterprise.

Lisa Ratner is wearing the Baby Seal. She and her sister Suzy,
who is modelling the Guinea Pig and the Rabbit, were tremen-
dously helpful and enthusiastic, and loved wearing their Beastly
Knits.

The Polar Bear is among the easiest to knit, and there is very
little embroidery to worry about, just a French knot for the eye and
a few chain stitches for a nose. The Baby Seal, too, is easy except
for the eyes, which are complicated. I've embroidered around the
pupils in chain stitch and highlighted the eyes in white. The dots on
either side of its nose are made with French knots, and the nostrils
with little half-circles of chain or back stitch.

49

INSTRUCTIONS: POLAR BEAR

MATERIALS
17x20g Texere Yarns 50/50 silk/wool mix in Ice Blue (No. 1822)
2x20g Texere Yarns 50/50 silk/wool mix in White (No. 1824)
1x20g Texere Yarns 50/50 silk/wool mix in Cream (No. 1827)
One pair each 3mm (No. 2) and 3¾mm (No. 4) knitting needles
One row counter
One stitch holder
One crochet hook

TENSION
26 stitches and 33 rows to 10cm x 10cm (4in) on size 3¾mm (No. 4) needles in St. st. It is important that your tension sample measures exactly the above dimensions to ensure size of sweater. If you have less stitches use a smaller needle, if more stitches use a larger needle.

MEASUREMENTS
Chest   112cm (44in)
Length   61cm (24in)
Sleeve seam   51cm (20in)

COLOUR CODING
The following instructions refer to the colours as shown here:
A Ice Blue (background)
B White
C Cream

PREPARATION
Divide one of the White balls in half, and the Cream in half.

ABBREVIATIONS
K   knit.
P   purl.
st.   stitch.
sts   stitches.

St.st.   Stocking stitch, (one row knit, one row purl alternately).
inc.   increase one stitch by working same stitch twice.
dec.   decrease by working 2 stitches together.
K2tog.   knit 2 stitches together.
P2tog.   purl 2 stitches together.
PU1   pick up the loop between the needles and place on left needle. Work this loop as an extra stitch.

FRONT
With colour A and 3mm (No. 2) needles cast on 140sts. In single rib (K1, P1) work 30 rows.
Changing to 3¾mm (No. 4) needles, K13, PU1, K6, PU1, *K6, PU1. Repeat from * 17 times, K13 (160sts).
Row 2–20: Work in St. st. starting with a P row.
Turn row counter to 0.

Start Pattern
Row 1: K124A, K5C, K31A.
Row 2: P30A, P10C, P120A.
Row 3: K117A, K14C, K29A.
Row 4: P22A, P23C, P115A.
Row 5: K115A, K24C, K21A.

These five rows set the position of the pattern. Now follow the graph from here to Row 130.
Adjust row counter to Row 150.
Row 151–170: Work in St. st.

Shape Neck
Row 171: K65, K2tog. Slip next 26sts on to the stitch holder. Join new colour A and K2tog. K65.

Row 172: P64, P2tog. On other side of neck P2tog. P64.
Repeat these two rows, decreasing one st. at both sides of neck edge, on the next 12 rows (53sts on either side).
Row 185–194: Work in St. st. on both sides of neck.

Shape Shoulders
Row 195: Cast off 13sts. K40. K other side of neck.
Row 196: Cast off 13sts. P40. P other side of neck.
Row 197: Cast off 13sts. K27. K other side of neck.
Row 198: Cast off 13sts. P27. P other side of neck.
Row 199: Cast off 13sts. K14. K other side of neck.
Row 200: Cast off 13sts. P14. P other side of neck.
Row 201: Cast off 14sts. K other side of neck.
Row 202: Cast off remaining 14sts.

FRONT NECK BAND
With colour A, 3mm (No. 2) needles and right side facing, pick up and knit from top left-hand side of neck, 32sts. In single rib (K1, P1) work the 26sts from stitch holder. Then pick up and knit 32sts from the right side of neck. Work in single rib for a further 7 rows.
Cast off loosely in rib.

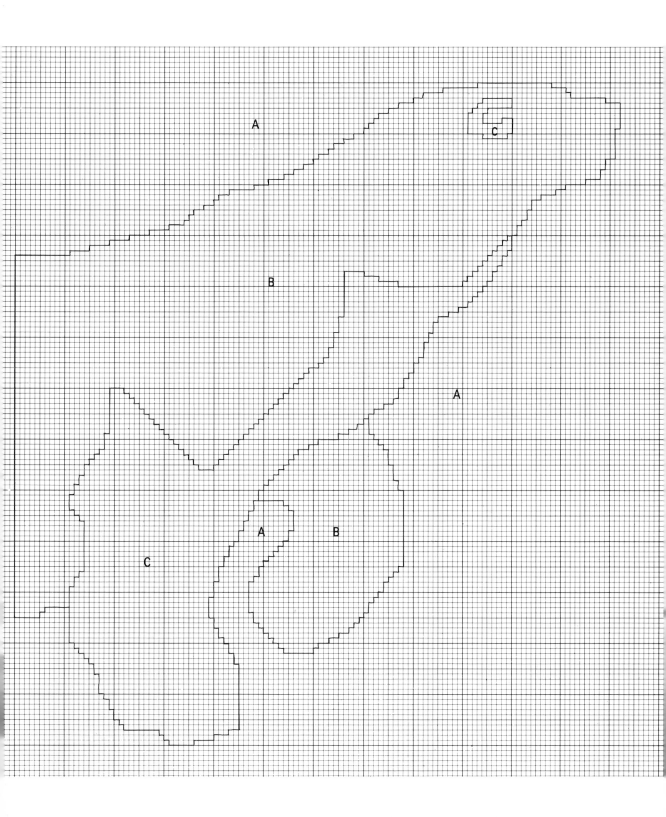

BACK

With colour A and 3mm (No. 2) needles cast on 140sts. In single rib (K1, P1) work 30 rows.
Changing to 3¾mm (No. 4) needles K13, PU1, K6, PU1, *K6, PU1. Repeat from * 17 times, K13 (160sts).
Row 2–20: Work in St. st. starting with a P row.
Turn row counter to 0.

Start Pattern

Row 1: K50A, K34C, K76A.
Row 2: P75A, P35C, P50A.
Row 3: K50A, K36C, K74A.
Row 4: P73A, P37C, P50A.
Row 5: K50A, K38C, K72A.

These five rows set the position of the pattern. Now follow the graph from here to Row 106.
Adjust row counter to Row 126.
Row 127–194: Work in St. st.

Shape Shoulders

Row 195: Cast off 13sts. K to end of row.
Row 196: Cast off 13sts. P to end of row.
Row 197: Cast off 13sts. K to end of row.
Row 198: Cast off 13sts. P to end of row.
Row 199: Cast off 13sts. K to end of row.
Row 200: Cast off 13sts. P to end of row.
Row 201: Cast off 14sts. K to end of row.
Row 202: Cast off 14sts. P to end of row.

BACK NECK BAND

Changing to 3mm (No. 2) needles, work 8 rows single rib on remaining 54sts.
Cast off loosely in rib.

SLEEVES (both alike)

With colour A and 3mm (No. 2) needles cast on 66sts.
In single rib work 30 rows.
Changing to 3¾mm (No. 4) needles, and working in St. st., increase one st. at both ends of the first row, the 4th row, the 8th row and every following 4th row until Row 132 (134sts).
Work a further 8 rows.
Cast off loosely.

EMBROIDERY

Refer to the chapter headed The Nature of the Beast, and embroider an eye and the nose.

MAKING UP

Using the crochet hook, work the loose ends of the yarn through the back of several sts of their own colour, to secure. Do not make knots.
On a flat surface, carefully pin out to size and press each piece.
Do not press the ribbing.
Pin and sew together the shoulder seams. Find the centre of each sleeve top, line up with shoulder seam. Pin into place and sew, ensuring both armhole side seams are of equal length.
Pin side and sleeve seams together and sew.
Press seams gently.

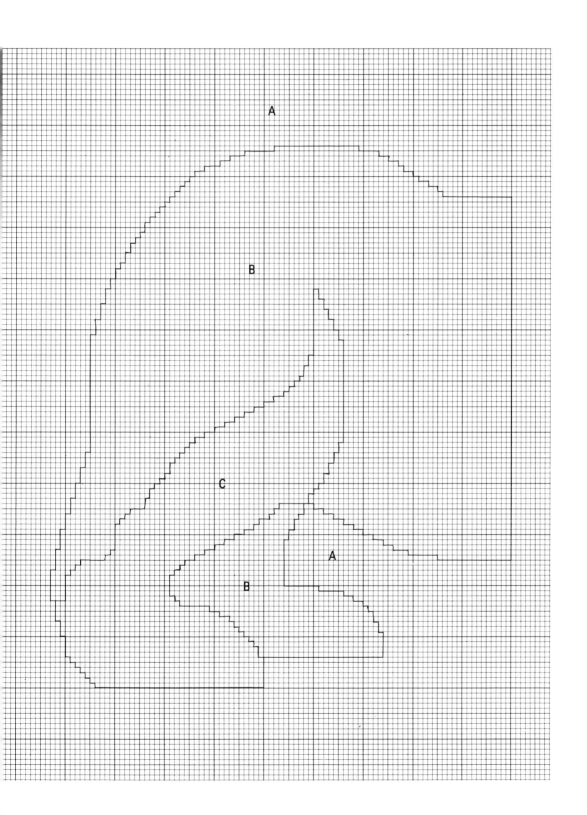

A

B

B

C

A

B

55

INSTRUCTIONS: BABY SEAL

MATERIALS
10x20g Texere Yarns 50/50 silk/wool mix in Ice Blue (No.1822)
2x20g Jaeger angora in White (No.550)
1x20g Jaeger angora in Fawn (No.557)
1x25g each of Patricia Roberts fine cotton in Charcoal Grey and Black
One pair each of 3mm (No.2) and 3¾mm (No.4) knitting needles
One row counter
One stitch holder
One crochet hook

TENSION
26 stitches and 33 rows to 10cm x 10cm (4in) on size 3¾mm (No.4) needles in St.st. It is important that your tension sample measures exactly the above dimensions to ensure size of sweater. If you have less stitches use a smaller needle, if more stitches use a larger needle.

MEASUREMENTS
Chest	86cm (34in)
Length	46cm (18in)
Sleeve seam	38cm (15in)

COLOUR CODING
The following instructions refer to the colours as shown here:
A Ice Blue (background)
B White
C Fawn
D Charcoal Grey
E Black

PREPARATION
Divide both balls of White in half, divide the Fawn into three, the Charcoal Grey into four balls, and the Black into two balls.

ABBREVIATIONS
K	knit.
P	purl.
st.	stitch.
sts	stitches.
St.st.	Stocking stitch, (knit one row, purl one row alternately).
inc.	increase one stitch by working same stitch twice.
dec.	decrease by working 2 stitches together.
K2tog.	knit 2 stitches together.
P2tog.	purl 2 stitches together.

FRONT
With colour A and 3mm (No.2) needles cast on 120sts. In single rib (K1,P1) work 25 rows.
Changing to 3¾mm (No.4) needles, work 4 rows in St.st. starting with a K row. Turn row counter to 0.

Start Pattern
Row 1: K9A, K26B, K85A.
Row 2: P81A, P29B, P10A.
Row 3: K11A, K30B, K79A.
Row 4: P79A, P29B, P12A.
Row 5: K12A, K30B, K78A.
Row 6: P19A, P24B, P34A, P30B, P13A.

These six rows set the position of the pattern. Now follow the graph from here to Row 92.
Adjust row counter to Row 96.
Row 97–130: Work in St.st.

Shape Neck
Row 131: K46, K2tog. Slip next 24sts on to the stitch holder. Join new colour A and K2tog. K46.
Row 132: P45, P2tog. On other side of neck P2tog. P45.

Repeat these two rows, decreasing one st. at both sides of neck edge, on the next 8 rows (38sts on either side).
Row 141–148: Work in St.st. on both sides of neck.

Shape Shoulders
Row 149: Cast off 12sts. K26. K other side of neck.
Row 150: Cast off 12sts. P26. P other side of neck.
Row 151: Cast off 12sts. K14. K other side of neck.
Row 152: Cast off 12sts. P14. P other side of neck.
Row 153: Cast off 14sts. K other side of neck.
Row 154: Cast off remaining 14sts.

FRONT NECK BAND
With colour A, 3mm (No.2) needles and right side facing, pick up and knit from top left-hand side of neck, 24sts. In single rib (K1,P1) work the 24sts from stitch holder. Then pick up and knit 24sts from the right side of neck. Work in single rib for a further 7 rows.
Cast off loosely in rib.

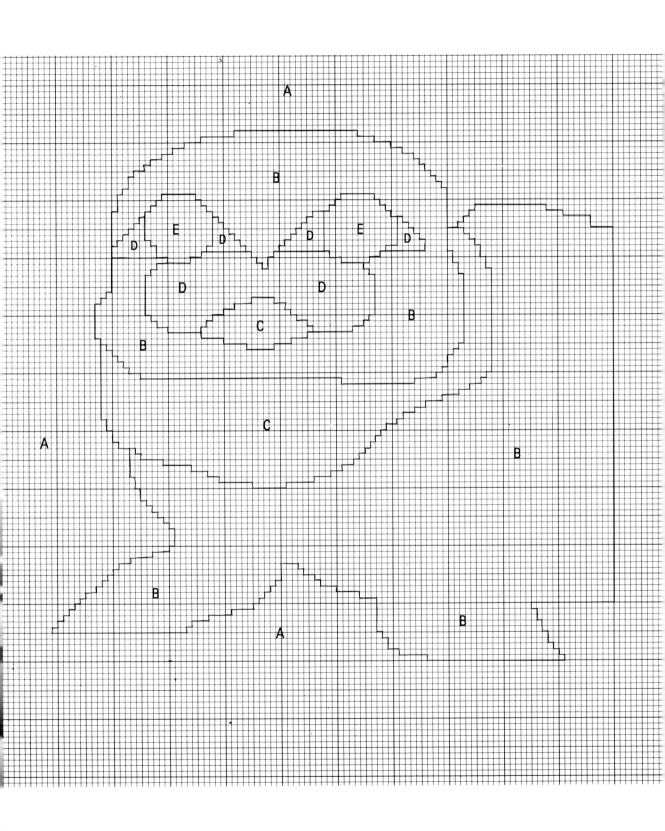

BACK

With colour A and 3mm (No. 2) needles cast on 120 sts. In single rib (K1, P1) work 25 rows.
Changing to 3¾mm (No. 4) needles, and starting with a K row, work 14 rows in St. st. Turn row counter to 0.

Start Pattern

Row 1: K114A, K6B.
Row 2: P10B, P110A.
Row 3: K108A, K12B.
Row 4: P14B, P106A.
Row 5: K104A, K16B.

These five rows set the position of the pattern. Now follow the graph from here to Row 103.
Adjust row counter to Row 107.
Row 108–148: Work in St. st.

Shape Shoulders

Row 149: Cast off 12 sts. K to end of row.
Row 150: Cast off 12 sts. P to end of row.
Row 151: Cast off 12 sts. K to end of row.
Row 152: Cast off 12 sts. P to end of row.
Row 153: Cast off 14 sts. K to end of row.
Row 154: Cast off 14 sts. P to end of row.

BACK NECK BAND

Changing to 3mm (No. 2) needles, work 8 rows single rib on remaining 44 sts.
Cast off loosely in rib.

SLEEVES (both alike)

With colour A and 3mm (No. 2) needles cast on 60 sts. In single rib work 25 rows.
Changing to 3¾mm (No. 4) needles and working in St. st., increase one st. at

both ends of the first row, the 4th row, the 8th row and every following 4th row until Row 96 (110 sts).
Work 4 more rows in St. st. Cast off loosely.

EMBROIDERY

Refer to the chapter headed The Nature of the Beast, and embroider features. (The line on the graph on the Charcoal Grey is a guide for the embroidery.)

MAKING UP

Using the crochet hook, work the loose ends of the yarn through the back of several sts of their own colour, to secure. Do not make knots.
On a flat surface, carefully pin out to size and press each piece.
Do not press the ribbing.
Pin and sew together the shoulder seams. Find the centre of each sleeve top, line up with shoulder seam. Pin into place and sew, ensuring both armhole side seams are of equal length.
Pin side and sleeve seams together and sew.
Press seams gently.

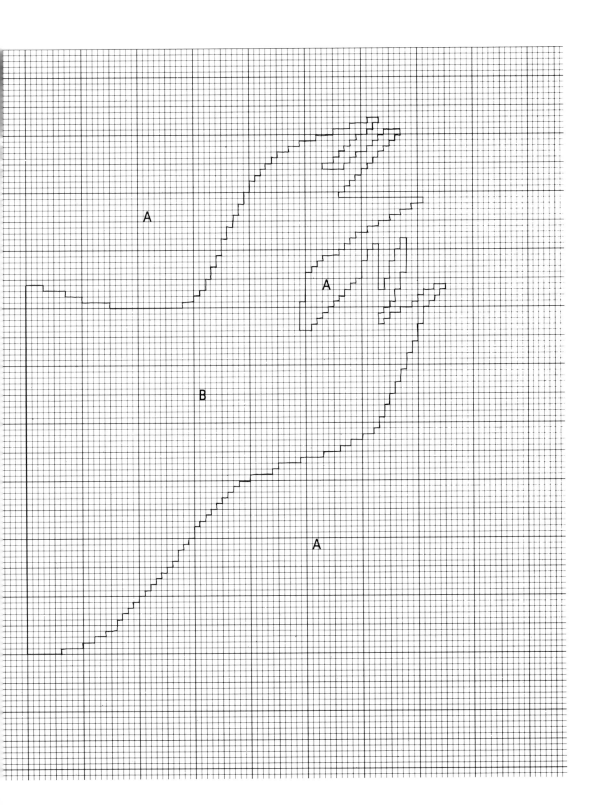

59

BADGER

All the non-knitted animals in this book belong to my mother, who is wearing the Beastly Badger for this photograph. She has the most fabulous private collection of carved wooden fairground animals, as you can see from these pictures, and was incredibly patient and kind to let us take over her flat for several days in order to give this knitting book quite the most original backgrounds ever. It seems rather silly that I should have chosen to ask her to wear one of the few animals that does not have a carved counterpart in her collection, but she especially liked the Badger, so here she is on her own.

I think the badger is one of those animals loved by everyone, and that this sweater could be worn equally well by men or women. Did you know, by the way, that badgers drag bits of grass, leaves and hay down into their setts and sometimes, in the morning, they take these makeshift mattresses out into the sunshine to air? I thought you would be interested in that useless piece of information. They are generally nocturnal animals, so perhaps you should only wear this sweater at night. And, if you want to be really zoologically accurate, you had better knit several sweaters and go around in a group. Badgers are highly gregarious.

It is not a very difficult sweater to knit, except for the face and those white bits for the ears. The eyes and nose are very simple to add – see The Nature of the Beast chapter.

INSTRUCTIONS: BADGER

MATERIALS
8x50g Jaeger alpaca in Slate (No.381)
1x50g each Jaeger alpaca in Black (No.312), White (No.142)
1x25g Nina Miklin Vogue wool in Grey (No.933)
One pair each 2¼mm (No.0) and 2¾mm (No.1) knitting needles
One row counter
One crochet hook

TENSION
25 stitches and 35 rows to 10cm x 10cm (4in) on size 2¾mm (No.1) needles in St.st. It is important that your tension sample measures exactly the above dimensions to ensure size of sweater. If you have less stitches use a smaller needle, if more stitches use a larger needle.

MEASUREMENTS
Chest	119cm (47in)
Length	63cm (25in)
Sleeve seam	63cm (25in)

COLOUR CODING
The following instructions refer to the colours as shown here:
A Slate (background)
B Grey
C Black
D White

PREPARATION
Divide Grey into three balls, Black into four balls and White into four balls.

ABBREVIATIONS
K	knit.
P	purl.
st.	stitch.
sts	stitches.
St.st.	Stocking stitch, (one row knit, one row purl alternately).
inc.	increase by working into same stitch twice.
dec.	decrease by working 2 stitches together.
K2tog.	knit 2 stitches together.
P2tog.	purl 2 stitches together.
PU1	pick up the loop between the needles and place on left needle. Work this loop as an extra stitch.

FRONT
With colour A and 2¼mm (No.0) needles cast on 140sts. In single rib (K1,P1) work 30 rows.
Changing to 2¾mm (No.1) needles K13, PU1, *K13, PU1. Repeat from * 8 times, K10 (150sts).
Row 2–50: Work in St.st. starting with a P row.
Turn row counter to 0.

Start Pattern
Row 1: K51A, K5C, K39A, K10C, K45A.
Row 2: P42A, P14C, P37A, P12C, P45A.
Row 3: K45A, K15C, K33A, K17C, K40A.
Row 4: P37A, P20C, P31A, P17C, P45A.
Row 5: K45A, K18C, K30A, K22C, K35A.

These five rows set the position of the pattern. Now follow the graph from here to Row 96.
Adjust row counter to Row 136.
Row 137–145: Work in St.st.

Neck Shaping
Row 146: P73, P2tog. Join new colour A and P2tog. P73.
Row 147: K74sts on both sides of neck.
Row 148: P72, P2tog. On other side of neck P2tog. P72.
Row 149: K73sts on both sides of neck.
Row 150–199: Continue to dec. one st. at neck edge of every P row (48sts).

Shape Shoulders
Row 200: Still continuing to dec. as above on the neck edge, cast off 12sts. P to end of both sides.
Row 201: Cast off 12sts. K to end of both sides.
Row 202: Cast off 11sts. P to end of both sides.
Row 203: Cast off 11sts. K to end of both sides.
Row 204: Cast off 11sts. P to end of both sides.
Row 205: Cast off 11sts. K to end of both sides.
Row 206: Cast off 11sts. Purl other side of neck.
Row 207: Cast off remaining 10sts.

FRONT NECK BAND
With colour A, 2¼mm (No.0) needles and right side facing, pick up and knit 62sts. from top left-hand side of neck. Work in single rib (K1,P1) for 7 rows, decreasing one st. (by K2tog.) at point of V as follows:
At end of Row 3, 5 and 7, K2tog.
At beginning of Row 4 and 6, K2tog. (57sts).
Cast off loosely in rib.
Repeat for right-hand side of neck, but with wrong side facing, pick up and knit 62sts.

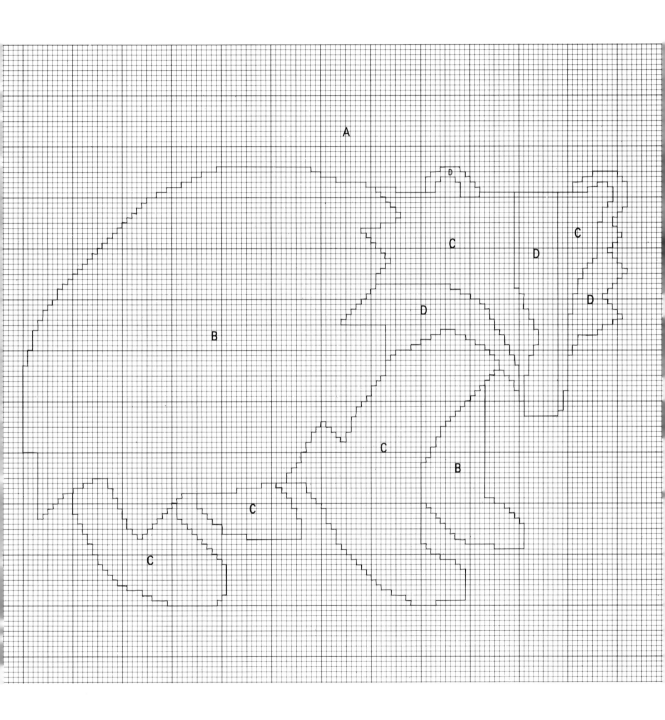

A

D

C

D

C

B

D

C

B

C

C

C

63

BACK

With colour A and 2¼mm (No.0) needles cast on 140sts. In single rib (K1,P1) work 30 rows.
Changing to 2¾mm (No.1) needles, K13, PU1, *K13, PU1. Repeat from * 8 times, K10 (150sts).
Row 2–199: Work in St.st. starting with a P row.

Shape Shoulders

Row 200: Cast off 12sts. P to end of row.
Row 201: Cast off 12sts. K to end of row.
Row 202: Cast off 11sts. P to end of row.
Row 203: Cast off 11sts. K to end of row.
Row 204: Cast off 11sts. P to end of row.
Row 205: Cast off 11sts. K to end of row.
Row 206: Cast off 11sts. P to end of row.
Row 207: Cast off 11sts. K to end of row.

BACK NECK BAND

Changing to 2¼mm (No.0) needles, work 8 rows single rib on remaining 60sts.
Cast off loosely in rib.

SLEEVES (both alike)

With colour A and 2¼mm (No.0) needles cast on 66sts. In single rib work 30 rows.
Changing to 2¾mm (No.1) needles, and working in St.st., inc. one st. at both ends of the first row, the 4th row, the 8th row and every following 4th row until Row 156 (146sts).
Work 4 more rows in St.st. Cast off loosely.

EMBROIDERY

Refer to the chapter headed The Nature of the Beast, and embroider two eyes and the tip of the nose.

MAKING UP

Using the crochet hook, work the loose ends of the yarn through the back of several sts of their own colour, to secure. Do not make knots.
Carefully sew together the ribbing at the point of the V neck, matching stitches.
On a flat surface, carefully pin out to size and press each piece.
Do not press the ribbing.
Sew together the shoulder seams. Find the centre of each sleeve top and line up with shoulder seam. Pin into place and sew, ensuring both armhole side seams are of equal length. Pin side and sleeve seams together and sew.
Press seams gently.

CAT AND MOUSE & LION

Sally and Farooq Hussain look just great in these two sweaters; and how lucky we were that my mother's private collection included an animal as rare in fairground terms as a lion. Sally and Farooq are managing to show off the sweaters beautifully in spite of the carved upstager. Sally loved the Cat and Mouse, highly amused that on the front all you see is the little mouse and one threatening paw, and there, lurking around the corner, is the rest of an extremely predatory cat. This sweater is medium-difficult to do. The mouse looks rather odd until you have embroidered on his tail and claws and whiskers, and his eye. Until these have been added, you have got nothing but a grey blob. It's lovely transforming that blob into a mouse with just a few chain stitches and a bit of patience.

Patience is certainly needed for the Lion. Appropriately enough, this one has to fall into the Real Brute category, so concentrate like mad on the instructions and be careful not to muddle up the two shades of brown. As in other sweaters where we have used the very fine lurex, you will find that it adds to your problems and, unless you are feeling lion-hearted, leave it out. The brave knitters will be rewarded by the added glamour and the sense of achievement. I seem to have got rather bored with embroidering claws on the lion, and given the poor creature only two on one of his back paws. The claws can be left off altogether if you prefer, but I think they look good and are worth the extra time spent. The Lion's face is very easy: highlights for the eyes, a line of chain stitch following the top line of his pale chin, plus a line connecting up to his nose. The cat on the Cat and Mouse sweater needs its face and claws embroidering as shown in the photograph and described in The Nature of the Beast chapter.

INSTRUCTIONS: CAT AND MOUSE

MATERIALS
5x50g Yarnworks silk/cotton mix in Red
1x20g each of Jaeger angora in Fawn (No.557), Silver Grey (No.558) and White (No.550)
One pair each 2¾mm (No.1) and 3¼mm (No.3) knitting needles
One row counter
One stitch holder
One crochet hook

TENSION
26 stitches and 35 rows to 10cm x 10cm (4in) on size 3¼mm (No.3) needles in St.st. It is important that your tension sample measures exactly the above dimensions to ensure size of sweater. If you have less stitches use a smaller needle, if more stitches then use a larger needle.

MEASUREMENTS
Chest   101cm (40in)
Length   51cm (20in)
Sleeve seam   53cm (21in)

COLOUR CODING
The following instructions refer to the colours as shown here:
A Red (background)
B Fawn
C Silver Grey
D White

PREPARATION
Divide each angora ball into approximately three.

ABBREVIATIONS
K   knit.
P   purl.
st.   stitch.
sts   stitches.
St.st.   Stocking stitch, (one row knit, one row purl alternately).
inc.   increase one stitch by working twice into same stitch.
dec.   decrease by working 2 stitches together.
K2tog.   knit 2 stitches together.
P2tog.   purl 2 stitches together.
PU1   pick up the loop between the needles and place on left needle. Work this loop as an extra stitch.

FRONT
With colour A and 2¾mm (No.1) needles cast on 130sts. In single rib (K1,P1) work 25 rows.
Changing to 3¼mm (No.3) needles, K12, PU1, K12, PU1. Repeat 8 more times, finishing with K10 (140sts). Work 24 rows in St.st. starting with a P row.
Turn row counter to 0.

Start Pattern
Row 1: P60A, P9C, P3A, P5C, P3A, P4C, P56A.
Row 2: K57A, K4C, K1A, K7C, K1A, K10C, K60A.
Row 3: P61A, P21C, P58A.
Row 4: K57A, K22C, K61A.
Row 5: P62A, P21C, P57A.

These five rows set the position of the pattern. Now follow the graph from here to Row 32.
Adjust row counter to Row 57.
Row 58–136: Work in St.st.

Shape Neck
Row 137: K56, K2tog. Slip next 24sts on to the stitch holder. Join new colour A and K2tog. K56.
Row 138: P55, P2tog. On other side of neck P2tog. P55.
Repeat these two rows, decreasing one st. at both sides of neck edge, on the next 8 rows (48sts on either side of neck).
Row 147–156: Work in St.st. on both sides of neck.

Shape Shoulders
Row 157: Cast off 12sts. K36. K other side of neck.
Row 158: Cast off 12sts. P36. P other side of neck.
Row 159: Cast off 12sts. K24. K other side of neck.
Row 160: Cast off 12sts. P24. P other side of neck.
Row 161: Cast off 12sts. K12. K other side of neck.
Row 162: Cast off 12sts. P12. P other side of neck.
Row 163: Cast off 12sts. K other side of neck.
Row 164: Cast off remaining 12sts.

FRONT NECK BAND
With colour A, 2¾mm (No.1) needles and right side facing, pick up and knit from top left-hand side of neck, 28sts. In single rib (K1,P1) work the 24sts from stitch holder. Then pick up and knit 28sts from the right side of neck. Work in single rib for a further 7 rows.
Cast off loosely in rib.

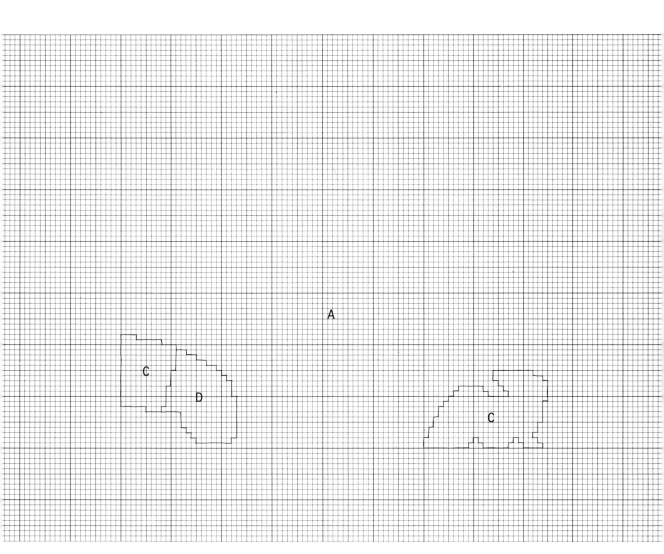

BACK

With colour A and 2¾mm (No.1) needles cast on 130sts. In single rib work 25 rows.

Changing to 3¼mm (No.3) needles, K12, PU1, K12, PU1. Repeat 8 times, K10 (140sts).

Row 2–25: Work in St.st. starting with a P row.

Turn row counter to 0.

Start Pattern

Row 1: P104A, P14D, P22A,
Row 2: K21A, K17D, K102A,
Row 3: P101A, P19D, P20A.
Row 4: K20A, K20D, K100A.
Row 5: P99A, P21D, P20A.

These five rows set the position of the pattern. Now follow the graph from here to Row 91.

Adjust row counter to Row 116.

Row 117–156: Work in St.st.

Shape Shoulders

Row 157: Cast off 12sts. K to end of row.
Row 158: Cast off 12sts. P to end of row.
Row 159: Cast off 12sts. K to end of row.
Row 160: Cast off 12sts. P to end of row.
Row 161: Cast off 12sts. K to end of row.
Row 162: Cast off 12sts. P to end of row.
Row 163: Cast off 12sts. K to end of row.
Row 164: Cast off 12sts. P to end of row.

BACK NECK BAND

Changing to 3¼mm (No.3) needles, work 8 rows single rib on remaining 44sts.
Cast off loosely in rib.

SLEEVES (both alike)

With colour A and 2¾mm (No.1) needles cast on 60sts. In single rib (K1,P1) work 25 rows.

Changing to 3¼mm (No.3) needles, and working in St.st., increase one st. at both ends of the first row, the 4th row, the 8th row and every following 4th row until Row 116 (120sts).

Work a further 4 rows.

Cast off loosely.

EMBROIDERY

Refer to the chapter headed The Nature of the Beast, and embroider features.

MAKING UP

Using the crochet hook, work the loose ends of the yarn through the back of several sts of their own colour, to secure. Do not make knots.

On a flat surface, carefully pin out to size and press each piece.

Do not press the ribbing.

Pin and sew together the shoulder seams. Find the centre of each sleeve top and line up with shoulder seam. Pin into place and sew, ensuring both armhole side seams are of equal length. Pin side and sleeve seams together and sew.

Press seams gently.

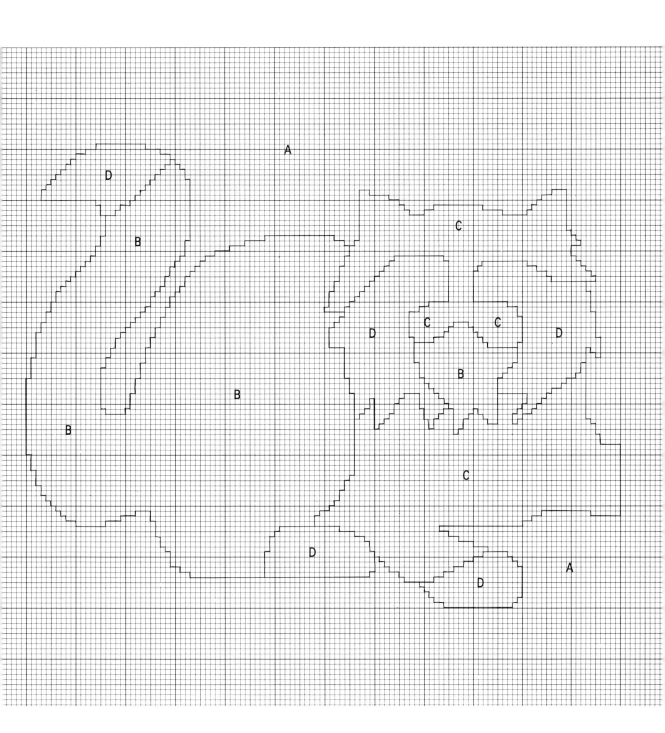

71

INSTRUCTIONS: LION

MATERIALS
8x50g Jaeger alpaca in Navy (Marina No. 344)
1x50g each of Jaeger Tan (Poncho No. 145) and White (Vicuna No. 146)
1x25g Nina Miklin Vogue wool in Dark Brown (No. 936)
1x25g Patricia Roberts fine cotton in Black (No. 8)
1 reel Nina Miklin fine lurex in Gold
One pair each 2¼mm (No. 0) and 3mm (No. 2) knitting needles
One row counter
One stitch holder
One crochet hook

TENSION
26 stitches and 34 rows to 10cm x 10cm (4in) on size 3mm (No. 2) needles in St. st. It is important that your tension sample measures exactly above dimensions to ensure size of sweater. If you have less stitches use a smaller needle, if more stitches then use a larger needle.

MEASUREMENTS
Chest   117cm (46in)
Length   61cm (24in)
Sleeve seam   58cm (23in)

COLOUR CODING
The following instructions refer to the colours as shown here:
A Navy (background)
B Tan
C Dark Brown (with lurex)
D Dark Brown
E White
F Black

PREPARATION
The Tan should be divided into five balls, the Dark Brown into two small balls with the remainder pre-wound with the Gold lurex into four/five small balls. Divide the White into two balls.

ABBREVIATIONS
K   knit.
P   purl.
st.   stitch.
sts   stitches.
St.st. Stocking stitch, (knit one row, purl one row alternately).
inc.   increase one stitch by working same stitch twice.
dec.   decrease by working 2 stitches together.
K2tog. knit 2 stitches together.
P2tog. purl 2 stitches together.
PU1   pick up the loop between the needles and place on left needle. Work this loop as an extra stitch.

FRONT
With colour A and 2¼mm (No. 0) needles cast on 140sts. In single rib (K1, P1) work 30 rows.
Changing to 3mm (No. 2) needles, K13, PU1, K6, PU1, *K6, PU1. Repeat from *17 times, K13 (160sts).
Row 2–10: Work in St. st. starting with a P row.
Turn row counter to 0.

Start Pattern
Row 1: K46A, K16B, K98A.
Row 2: P97A, P18B, P45A.
Row 3: K44A, K20B, K96A.
Row 4: P96A, P21B, P43A.
Row 5: K40A, K24B, K96A.

These five rows set the position of the pattern. Now follow the graph from here to Row 140.
Adjust row counter to Row 150.
Row 151–170: Work in St. st.

Shape Neck
Row 171: K63, K2tog. Slip next 26sts on to the stitch holder. Join new colour A and K2tog. K63.
Row 172: P61, P2tog. On other side of neck P2tog. P61.
Repeat these two rows, decreasing one st. at both sides of neck edge, on the next 10 rows (55sts on either side).
Row 183–194: Work in St. st. on both sides of neck.

Shape Shoulders
Row 195: Cast off 14sts. K41. K other side of neck.
Row 196: Cast off 14sts. P41. P other side of neck.
Row 197: Cast off 14sts. K27. K other side of neck.
Row 198: Cast off 14sts. P27. P other side of neck.
Row 199: Cast off 14sts. K13. K other side of neck.
Row 200: Cast off 14sts. P13. P other side of neck.
Row 201: Cast off 13sts. K other side of neck.
Row 202: Cast off remaining 13sts.

FRONT NECK BAND
With colour A, 2¼mm (No. 0) needles and right side facing, pick up and knit from top left-hand side of neck, 32sts. In single rib (K1, P1) work the 26sts from stitch holder. Then pick up and knit 32sts from the right side of neck. Work in single rib for a further 7 rows.
Cast off loosely in rib.

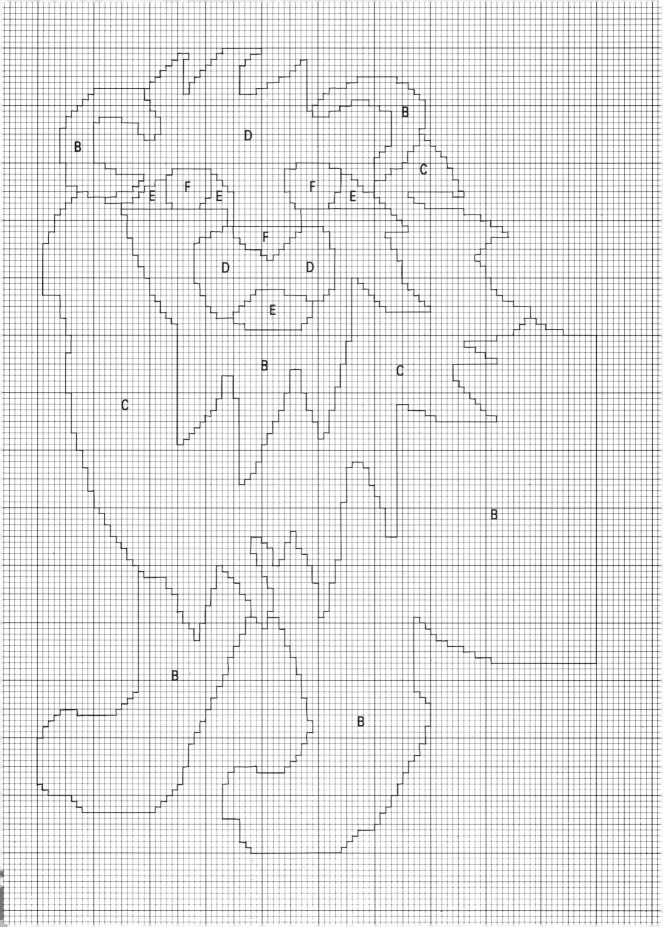

BACK

With colour A and 2¼mm (No.0) needles cast on 140sts. In single rib (K1,P1) work 30 rows.
Changing to 3mm (No.2) needles, K13, PU1, K6, PU1, *K6, PU1. Repeat from * 17 times, K13 (160sts).
Row 2–10: Work in St.st. starting with a P row.
Turn row counter to 0.

Start Pattern

Row 1: K85A, K20B, K55A.
Row 2: P54A, P22B, P84A.
Row 3: K83A, K24B, K53A.
Row 4: P52A, P26B, P82A.
Row 5: K81A, K27B, K52A.

These five rows set the position of the pattern. Now follow the graph from here to Row 135.
Adjust row counter to Row 145.
Row 146–194: Work in St.st.

Shape Shoulders

Row 195: Cast off 14sts. K to end of row.
Row 196: Cast off 14sts. P to end of row.
Row 197: Cast off 14sts. K to end of row.
Row 198: Cast off 14sts. P to end of row.
Row 199: Cast off 14sts. K to end of row.
Row 200: Cast off 14sts. P to end of row.
Row 201: Cast off 13sts. K to end of row.
Row 202: Cast off 13sts. P to end of row.

BACK NECK BAND

Changing to 2¼mm (No.0) needles, work 8 rows single rib on remaining 50sts.
Cast off loosely in rib.

SLEEVES (both alike)

With colour A and 2¼mm (No.0) needles cast on 66sts. In single rib work 30 rows.
Changing to 3mm (No.2) needles, and working in St.st., increase one st. at both ends of the first row, the 4th row, the 8th row and every following 4th row until Row 100 (118sts).
Thereafter increase at both ends of every 5th row until Row 150 (138sts).
Work 5 more rows St.st.
Cast off loosely.

EMBROIDERY

Refer to the chapter headed The Nature of the Beast, and embroider eyes, nose outline and claws.

MAKING UP

Using the crochet hook, work the loose ends of the yarn through the back of several sts of their own colour, to secure. Do not make knots.
On a flat surface, carefully pin out to size and press each piece.
Do not press the ribbing.
Pin and sew together the shoulder seams. Find the centre of each sleeve top and line up with shoulder seam. Pin into place and sew, ensuring both armhole side seams are of equal length.
Pin side and sleeve seams together and sew.
Press seams gently.

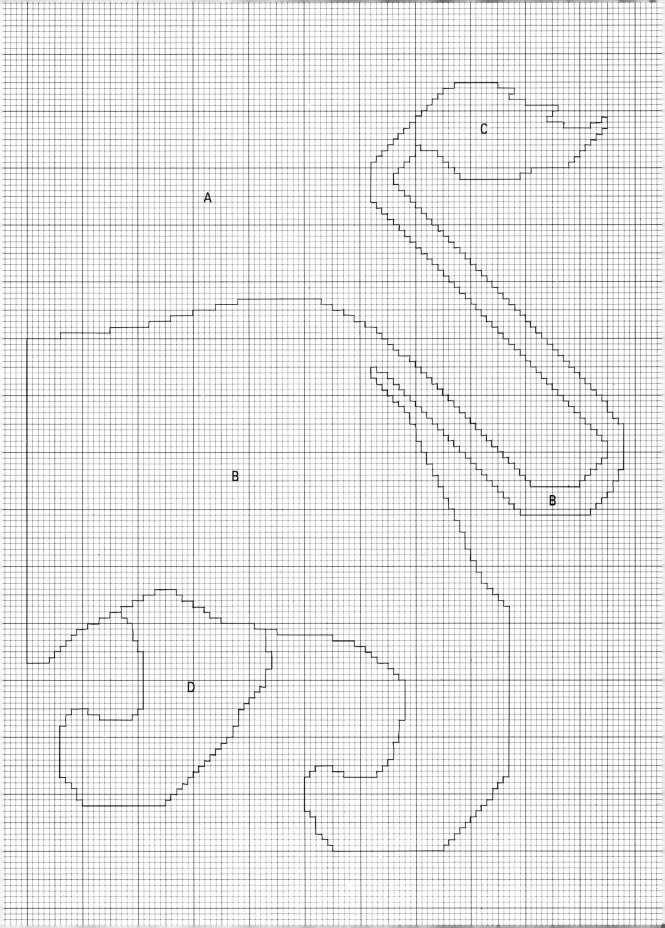

GUINEA PIG

Suzy Ratner is wearing the Guinea Pig and thought this sweater
was very funny. She loved the spiky mohair animal sticking out
from its cotton background. It's a sort of punk guinea pig. You can
amuse yourself making sure that the punky long bits of mohair are
knitted through to the right side of the animal, and you can fluff it
up a bit once you have finished. Don't go and squash the poor thing
with an iron – pressed-punk-pig is not a pretty sight.

The Guinea Pig does look rather like a curious abstract blob
until you add the little touches of embroidery. Then, suddenly, you
have an animal instead of a blob. It's extraordinary how a little
white eye, a nose and a few whiskers can bring the whole thing to
life. If you are an inexperienced knitter, you can embroider the
little feet rather than worry about knitting these slightly
complicated shapes. The feet are really the only difficult bit about
this sweater. The rest is fairly easy.

I've chosen a guinea pig because lots of children have them as
pets and those of the tortoise-shell variety are the most beautiful,
geometric little creatures. If you had an all-black guinea pig and
decided to adapt the design, I think you might have a bit more
trouble convincing people that you weren't wearing a big blob. So,
I think you should stick to my version and hope that your pet
doesn't take offence.

INSTRUCTIONS: GUINEA PIG

MATERIALS
12x25g Patricia Roberts fine cotton in Yellow (No.3)
1x25g Patricia Roberts fine cotton in Black (No.8)
1x25g each Patricia Roberts mohair in Black (No.21), Orange (No.7) and White (No.20)
One pair each 2¼mm (No.0) and 3mm (No.2) knitting needles
One row counter
One stitch holder
One crochet hook

TENSION
28 stitches and 36 rows to 10cm x 10cm (4in) on size 3mm (No.2) needles in St.st. It is important that your tension sample measures exactly the above dimensions to ensure size of sweater. If you have less stitches use a smaller needle, if more stitches then use a larger needle.

MEASUREMENTS
Chest   84cm (33in)
Length   51cm (20in)
Sleeve seam   43cm (17in)

COLOUR CODING
The following instructions refer to the colours as shown here:
A Yellow (background)
B Orange
C Black (mohair)
D White
E Black (cotton)

PREPARATION
Divide each mohair into three separate balls, and the Black cotton into six separate lengths of about 60cm (24in) long, for the feet.

ABBREVIATIONS
K   knit.
P   purl.
st.   stitch.
sts   stitches.
St.st.   Stocking stitch, (one row knit, one row purl alternately).
inc.   increase one stitch by working same stitch twice.
dec.   decrease by working 2 stitches together.
K2tog.   knit 2 stitches together.
P2tog.   purl 2 stitches together.
PU1   pick up the loop between the needles and place on left needle. Work this loop as an extra stitch.

FRONT
With colour A and 2¼mm (No.0) needles cast on 110sts. In single rib (K1,P1) work 25 rows.
Changing to 3mm (No.2) needles K10, PU1, K10, PU1. Repeat 8 more times, K10 (120sts).
Work a further 39 rows in St.st. starting with a P row. Turn row counter to 0.

Start Pattern
Row 1: K27A, K4E, K89A.
Row 2: P92A, P2E, P26A.
Row 3: K26A, K1E, K93A.
Row 4: P87A, P8E, P1D, P24A.
Row 5: K23A, K2D, K2E, K93A.
Row 6: P40A, P1E, P47A, P7E, P3D, P22A.

These six rows set the position of the pattern. Now follow the graph from here to Row 81.

Adjust row counter to Row 121.
Row 122–140: Work in St.st.

Shape Neck
Row 141: K48, K2tog. Slip next 20sts on to the stitch holder. Join new colour A and K2tog. K48.
Row 142: P47, P2tog. On other side of neck P2tog. P47.
Repeat these two rows, decreasing one st. at both sides of neck edge, on the next 10 rows (38sts on either side).
Row 153–164: Work in St.st. on both sides of neck.

Shape Shoulders
Row 165: Cast off 12sts. K26. K other side of neck.
Row 166: Cast off 12sts. P26. P other side of neck.
Row 167: Cast off 12sts. K14. K other side of neck.
Row 168: Cast off 12sts. P14. P other side of neck.
Row 169: Cast off 14sts. K other side of neck.
Row 170: Cast off remaining 14sts.

FRONT NECK BAND
With colour A, 2¼mm (No.0) needles and right side facing, pick up and knit from top left-hand side of neck, 30sts. In single rib (K1,P1) work the 20sts from stitch holder. Then pick up and knit 30sts from the right side of neck. Work in single rib for a further 7 rows.
Cast off loosely in rib.

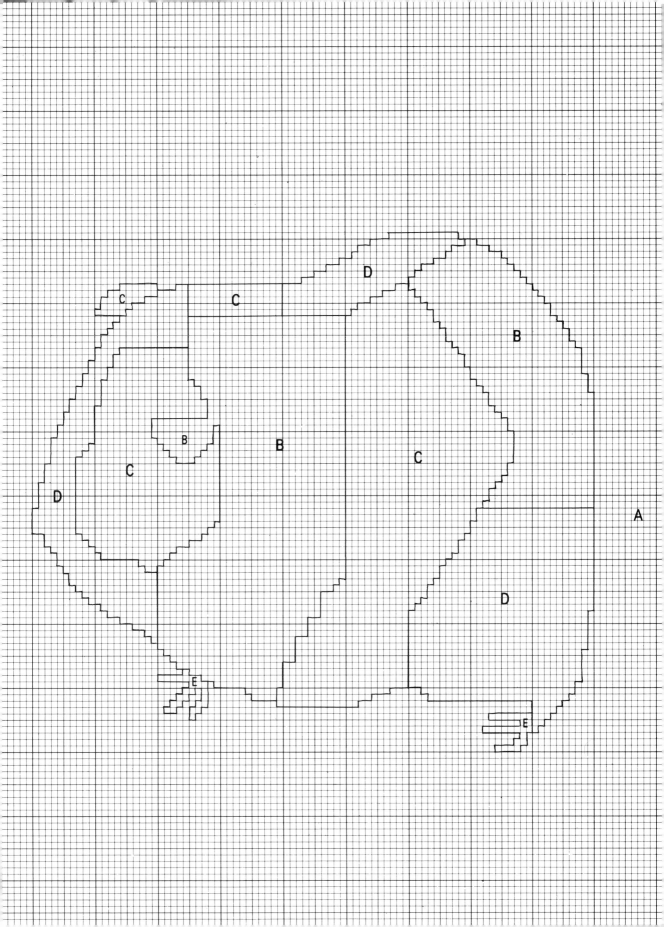

BACK

With colour A and 2¼mm (No. 0) needles cast on 110sts. In single rib (K1, P1) work 25 rows.
Changing to 3mm (No. 2) needles, K10, PU1, K10, PU1. Repeat 8 more times, K10 (120sts).
Row 2–164: Work in St. st. starting with a P row.

Shape Shoulders

Row 165: Cast off 12sts. K to end of row.
Row 166: Cast off 12sts. P to end of row.
Row 167: Cast off 12sts. K to end of row.
Row 168: Cast off 12sts. P to end of row.
Row 169: Cast off 14sts. K to end of row.
Row 170: Cast off 14sts. P to end of row.

BACK NECK BAND

Changing to 2¼mm (No. 0) needles, work 8 rows single rib on remaining 44sts.
Cast off loosely in rib.

SLEEVES (both alike)

With colour A and 2¼mm (No. 0) needles cast on 60sts. In single rib (K1, P1) work 25 rows.
Changing to 3mm (No. 2) needles, increase one st. at both ends of the first row, the 4th row, the 8th row and every following 4th row until Row 96 (110sts).
Work 4 further rows.
Cast off loosely.

EMBROIDERY

Refer to the chapter headed The Nature of the Beast, and embroider the eye, nose and whiskers.

MAKING UP

Using the crochet hook, work the loose ends of the yarn through the back of several sts of their own colour, to secure. Do not make knots.
On a flat surface, carefully pin out to size and press each piece.
Do not press the ribbing or the mohair pig.
Sew together the shoulder seams. Find the centre of each sleeve top and line up with shoulder seam. Pin into place and sew, ensuring both armhole side seams are of equal length. Pin side and sleeve seams together and sew.
Press seams gently.

KOALAS & KANGAROO

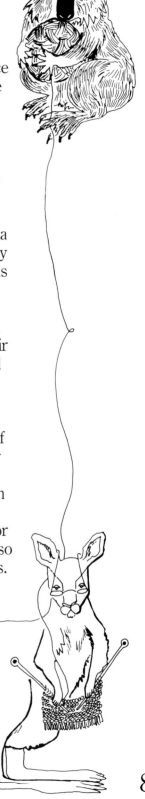

I love this photograph. I think it's my favourite, although the choice is almost impossible since my parents and all the friends who have been generous enough to give up their time and come to be photographed for my book have brought to life my designs and made the Beastly Knits look marvellous.

I don't think Andrew Chelley, who is three, and Charlotte Evans, who is six, particularly minded giving up their time to be photographed with a fairground giraffe for company rather than doing their homework. Andrew is perhaps a bit young for homework, but he had a very happy afternoon modelling the Koala Bears and said he liked them very much, especially the way they are holding hands. At least, I think he was referring to the koalas holding hands, but perhaps he meant the added attraction of holding hands with Charlotte.

I thought it would be rather unoriginal to have a koala with a baby riding on her back. They hardly ever come down from their eucalyptus tree, but this little one has fallen off and is being hauled along by its mother. You will understand the way the paws link by looking at the graph drawing rather than the photograph where, inevitably, it is less easy to see every detail.

Charlotte liked the pocket on the Kangaroo and had all sorts of good ideas as to what could usefully be stored there: like a baby kangaroo.

The embroidery is simple: two black circles of tiny chain stitch (see the chapter headed The Nature of the Beast), and a single white chain stitch in the centre of each for the eyes, repeated for the Baby Koala. The same goes for the Kangaroo, which will also need a nose and mouth, again made with small black chain stitches.

81

INSTRUCTIONS: KOALAS

MATERIALS

8x25g Patricia Roberts fine cotton in Green (No.5)
1x25g Patricia Roberts fine cotton in Black (No.8)
1x25g each of Nina Miklin Vogue wool in White/Grey (No.931), Dark Grey (No.933), Dark Brown (No.936)
One pair each 2¼mm (No.0) and 3mm (No.2) knitting needles
One row counter
One stitch holder
One crochet hook

TENSION

28 stitches and 36 rows to 10cm x 10cm (4in) on size 3mm (No.2) needles in St.st. It is important that your tension sample measures exactly above dimensions to ensure size of sweater. If you have less stitches use a smaller needle, if more stitches then use a larger needle.

MEASUREMENTS

Chest   76cm (30in)
Length   42cm (16½in)
Sleeve seam 33cm (13in)

COLOUR CODING

The following instructions refer to the colours as shown here:
A Green (background)
B White/Grey
C Dark Grey
D Dark Brown
E Black

PREPARATION

Divide the Dark Grey into three separate balls, with four long strands for the hand. Divide the White/Grey into four separate balls, and the Dark Brown in half.

ABBREVIATIONS

K	knit.
P	purl.
st.	stitch.
sts	stitches.
St.st.	Stocking stitch, (one row knit, one row purl alternately).
inc.	increase one stitch by working same stitch twice.
dec.	decrease by working 2 stitches together.
K2tog.	knit 2 stitches together.
P2tog.	purl 2 stitches together.

FRONT

With colour A and 2¼mm (No.0) needles cast on 110sts. In single rib (K1,P1) work 25 rows.
Changing to 3mm (No.2) needles, work 10 rows in St.st. starting with a K row. Turn row counter to 0.

Start Pattern

Row 1: K30A, K33C, K19D, K28A.
Row 2: P16A, P3C, P9A, P19D, P34C, P29A.
Row 3: K28A, K34C, K20D, K5A, K2C, K2A, K3C, K16A.
Row 4: P12A, P3C, P2A, P3C, P1A, P2C, P5A, P21D, P34C, P27A.
Row 5: K26A, K34C, K21D, K6A, K2C, K1A, K3C, K2A, K3C, K12A.

These five rows set the position of the pattern. Now follow the graph from here to Row 87.
Adjust row counter to Row 97.
Row 98–108: Work in St.st.

Shape Neck

Row 109: K43, K2tog. Slip next 20sts on to the stitch holder. Join new colour A and K2tog. K43.
Row 110: P42, P2tog. On other side of neck P2tog. P42.
Repeat the above two rows, decreasing one st. at both sides of neck edge, on the next 8 rows (35sts on either side).
Row 119–126: Work in St.st. on both sides of neck.

Shape Shoulders

Row 127: Cast off 12sts. K23. K other side of neck.
Row 128: Cast off 12sts. P23. P other side of neck.
Row 129: Cast off 12sts. K11. K other side of neck.
Row 130: Cast off 12sts. P11. P other side of neck.
Row 131: Cast off 11sts. K other side of neck.
Row 132: Cast off remaining 11sts.

FRONT NECK BAND

With colour A, 2¼mm (No.0) needles and right side facing, pick up and knit from top left-hand side of neck, 24sts. In single rib (K1,P1) work the 20sts from stitch holder. Then pick up and knit 24sts from the right side of neck. Work in single rib for a further 7 rows.
Cast off loosely in rib.

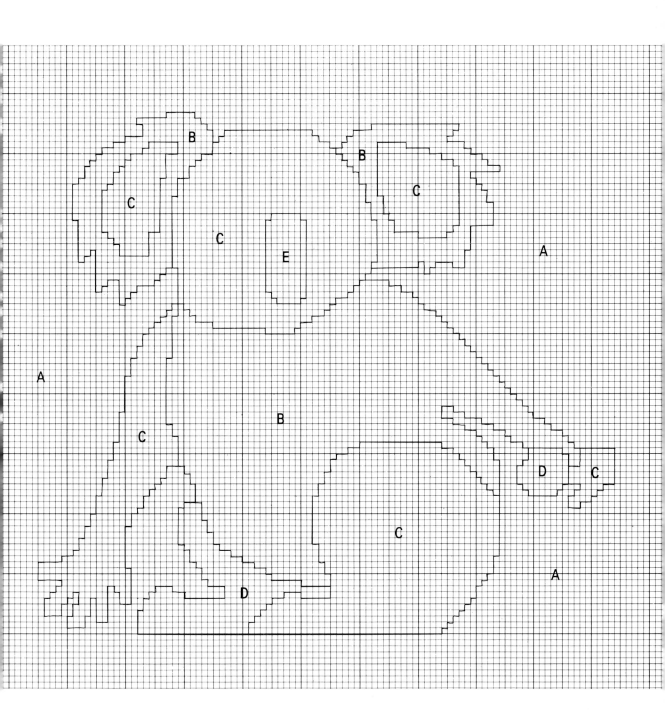

83

BACK

With colour A and 2¼mm (No.0) needles cast on 110sts. In single rib (K1,P1) work 25 rows.
Changing to 3mm (No.2) needles, and starting with a K row, work 10 rows in St.st. Turn row counter to 0.

Start Pattern

Row 1: K45A, K15D, K18A, K7B, K25A.
Row 2: P25A, P9B, P16A, P16D, P44A.
Row 3: K43A, K17D, K16A, K10B, K24A.
Row 4: P24A, P10B, P17A, P17D, P42A.
Row 5: K41A, K17D, K18A, K9B, K25A.

These five rows set the position of the pattern. Now follow the graph from here to Row 71.
Adjust row counter to Row 81.
Row 82–126: Work in St.st.

Shape Shoulders

Row 127: Cast off 12sts. K to end of row.
Row 128: Cast off 12sts. P to end of row.
Row 129: Cast off 12sts. K to end of row.
Row 130: Cast off 12sts. P to end of row.
Row 131: Cast off 11sts. K to end of row.
Row 132: Cast off 11sts. P to end of row.

BACK NECK BAND

Changing to 2¼mm (No.0) needles, work 8 rows single rib on remaining 40sts.
Cast off loosely in rib.

SLEEVES (both alike)

With colour A and 2¼mm (No.0) needles cast on 60sts.
In single rib (K1,P1) work 25 rows.
Changing to 3mm (No.2) needles, and working in St.st., increase one st. at both ends of the first row, the 4th row, the 8th row and every following 4th row until Row 76 (100sts).
Work a further 4 rows.
Cast off loosely.

EMBROIDERY

Refer to the chapter headed The Nature of the Beast, and embroider four eyes.

MAKING UP

Using the crochet hook, work the loose ends of the yarn through the back of several sts of their own colour, to secure. Do not make knots.
On a flat surface, carefully pin out to size and press each piece.
Do not press the ribbing.
Sew together the shoulder seams. Find the centre of each sleeve top and line up with shoulder seam. Pin into place and sew, ensuring both armhole side seams are of equal length. Pin side and sleeve seams together and sew.
Press seams gently.

INSTRUCTIONS: KANGAROO

MATERIALS
4x50g Jaeger alpaca in Wine Red (No.380)
1x50g each of Jaeger alpaca in Light Grey (Paloma No.148), Dark Grey (Plomo No.149), and Fawn (Vicuna No.146)
One pair each 2¼mm (No.0) and 3mm (No.2) knitting needles
One row counter
One stitch holder
One crochet hook

TENSION
26 stitches and 34 rows to 10cm x 10cm (4in) on size 3mm (No.2) needles in St.st. It is important that your tension sample measures exactly above dimensions to ensure size of sweater. If you have less stitches use a smaller needle, if more stitches then use a larger needle.

MEASUREMENTS
Chest	81cm (32in)
Length	46cm (18in)
Sleeve seam	38cm (15in)

COLOUR CODING
The following instructions refer to the colours as shown here:
A Wine Red (background)
B Dark Grey
C Light Grey
D Fawn

PREPARATION
Divide the Dark Grey into three balls, the Light Grey into two balls, the Fawn into three balls.

ABBREVIATIONS
K	knit.
P	purl.
st.	stitch.
sts	stitches.
St.st.	Stocking stitch, (one row knit, one row purl alternately).
inc.	increase one stitch by working same stitch twice.
dec.	decrease by working 2 stitches together.
K2tog.	knit 2 stitches together.
P2tog.	purl 2 stitches together.
PU1	pick up the loop between the needles and place on left needle. Work this loop as an extra stitch.

FRONT
With colour A and 2¼mm (No.0) needles cast on 100sts. In single rib (K1,P1) work 25 rows.
Changing to 3mm (No.2) needles, K9, PU1, K9, PU1. Repeat 8 more times, K10 (110sts).
Work one row P.
Turn row counter to 0.

Start Pattern
Row 1: K42A, K36B, K23A, K9B.
Row 2: P10B, P21A, P36B, P43A.
Row 3: K44A, K36B, K19A, K11B.
Row 4: P12B, P17A, P36B, P45A.
Row 5: K46A, K36B, K15A, K13B.

These five rows set the position of the pattern. Now follow the graph from here to Row 105.
Adjust row counter to Row 107.
Row 108–110: Work in St.st.

Shape Neck
Row 111: K43, K2tog. Slip next 20sts on to the stitch holder. Join new colour A and K2tog. K43.
Row 112: P42, P2tog. On other side of neck P2tog. P42.
Repeat these two rows, decreasing one st. at both sides of neck edge, on the next 8 rows (35sts on either side).
Row 121–128: Work in St.st. on both sides of neck.

Shape Shoulders
Row 129: Cast off 12sts. K23. K other side of neck.
Row 130: Cast off 12sts. P23. P other side of neck.
Row 131: Cast off 12sts. K11. K other side of neck.
Row 132: Cast off 12sts. P11. P other side of neck.
Row 133: Cast off 11sts. K other side of neck.
Row 134: Cast off remaining 11sts.

FRONT NECK BAND
With colour A, 2¼mm (No.0) needles and right side facing, pick up and knit from top left-hand side of neck, 24sts.
In single rib (K1,P1) work the 20sts from stitch holder. Then pick up and knit 24sts from the right side of neck. Work in single rib for a further 7 rows.
Cast off loosely in rib.

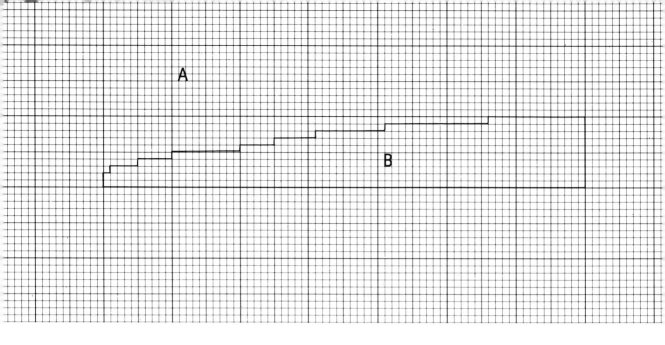

BACK

With colour A and 2¼mm (No.0) needles cast on 100sts. In single rib (K1,P1) work 25 rows.
Changing to 3mm (No.2) needles, K9, PU1, K9, PU1. Repeat 8 more times, K10 (110sts).
Row 2: P to end of row.
Turn row counter to 0.

Start Pattern

Row 1: K70B, K40A.
Row 2: P40A, P70B.
Row 3: K69B, K41A.
Row 4: P45A, P65B.
Row 5: K60B, K50A.

Row 6–10: Follow graph as set.
Turn row counter to Row 12.
Row 13–128: Work in St.st.

Shape Shoulders

Row 129: Cast off 12sts. K to end of row.
Row 130: Cast off 12sts. P to end of row.
Row 131: Cast off 12sts. K to end of row.
Row 132: Cast off 12sts. P to end of row.
Row 133: Cast off 11sts. K to end of row.

Row 134: Cast off 11sts. P to end of row.

BACK NECK BAND

Changing to 2¼mm (No.0) needles, work 8 rows single rib on remaining 40sts.
Cast off loosely in rib.

SLEEVES (both alike)

With colour A and 2¼mm (No.0) needles cast on 60sts. In single rib (K1,P1) work 25 rows.
Changing to 3mm (No.2) needles, and working in St.st., increase one st. at both ends of the first row, the 4th row, the 8th row and every following 4th row until Row 96 (110sts).
Work a further 4 rows.
Cast off loosely.

POUCH

With colour D and 3mm (No.2) needles cast on 40sts. Working in single rib throughout, follow the area for the pouch on the graph, increasing or decreasing where necessary, until Row 25.
Change to 2¼mm (No.0)

needles and work 7 rows single rib.
Cast off loosely in rib.

EMBROIDERY

Refer to the chapter headed The Nature of the Beast, and embroider the eyes and nose.

MAKING UP

Using the crochet hook, work the loose ends of the yarn through the back of several sts of their own colour, to secure. Do not make knots.
On a flat surface, carefully pin out to size and press each piece.
Do not press the ribbing.
Pin the pouch to the outline of the pouch on the sweater front, and oversew in position. Sew together the shoulder seams. Find the centre of each sleeve top and line up with shoulder seam. Pin into place and sew, ensuring both armhole side seams are of equal length. Pin side and sleeve seams together and sew.
Press seams gently.

TURTLE

I based this Turtle on something called the False Map Turtle, which sounds even better in its Latin version: *Graptemys pseudographica*. So, it could be described as a sort of mock turtle and we've given the sweater a mock turtle neckline to match. The False Map Turtle does have some rather curious habits. For instance, I learn from my animal encyclopedia that during courtship the False Male, who is the smaller of the two, bashes the False Female on the snout with his feet. I thought you might like that useless piece of turtle-lore, and I hope you are as brave as the male *pseudographica* when it comes to tackling this sweater. It isn't all that easy.

We asked Zella Fuller to wear the sweater, and she really does look wonderful, doesn't she? And on top of looking wonderful, on the day that she came to model for Beastly Knits, she was endlessly patient and generous about allowing the fairground cockerel to get in on the act.

Having lulled you into a false sense of security, I shall get back to the Real Brutishness of this sweater. The feet are difficult, but please don't give up. There's a real treat in store when you get to the shell: I'm afraid it's the superfine lurex again, which really can't be used separately from the yarn but must be pre-wound with the yarn before starting to knit, or you will find it will float off all over the place because it's so fine.

If you can't face all the extra work involved, or if you find the lurex hard to get hold of, don't worry. Just leave it out. The extra sparkle is nice but it certainly isn't by any means essential. The embroidery is the easiest part – just a black chain stitch circle for the eye with a white dot for the highlight. See The Nature of the Beast chapter.

91

INSTRUCTIONS: TURTLE

MATERIALS
6x50g Yarnworks silk/cotton mix in Red
1x25g each of Patricia Roberts fine cotton in Green (No.5), Black (No.8) and Khaki (No.2)
1 reel Nina Miklin fine lurex in Bronze (optional)
One pair each 2¼mm (No.0) and 3¼mm (No.3) knitting needles
One row counter
One crochet hook

TENSION
26 stitches and 35 rows to 10cm x 10cm (4in) on size 3¼mm (No.3) needles in St.st. It is important that your tension sample measures exactly the above dimensions to ensure size of sweater. If you have less stitches use a smaller needle, if more stitches use a larger needle.

MEASUREMENTS
Chest   101cm (40in)
Length   62cm (24½in)
Sleeve seam 51cm (20in)

COLOUR CODING
The following instructions refer to the colours as shown here:
A Red (background)
B Green
C Black
D Khaki

PREPARATION
Divide the Black into four balls and the Green into three balls. The optional Bronze fine lurex only used in the Turtle's shell and must be pre-wound with the green and black. Wind the Khaki into lots of little balls (see the Turtle's feet).

ABBREVIATIONS
K	knit.
P	purl.
st.	stitch.
sts	stitches.
St.st.	Stocking stitch, (one row knit, one row purl alternately).
inc.	increase one stitch by working into same stitch twice.
dec.	decrease by working 2 stitches together.
K2tog.	knit 2 stitches together.
P2tog.	purl 2 stitches together.
PU1	pick up the loop between the needles and place on left needle. Work this loop as an extra stitch.

FRONT
With colour A and 2¼mm (No.0) needles cast on 130sts. In single rib (K1,P1) work 30 rows.
Changing to 3¼mm (No.3) needles, K12, PU1, K12, PU1. Repeat 8 times, K10 (140sts).
Work 23 rows in St.st. starting with a P row.
Turn row counter to 0.

Start Pattern
Row 1: K81A, K5C, K1D, K53A.
Row 2: P52A, P2D, P6C, P80A.
Row 3: K77A, K9C, K4D, K50A.
Row 4: P53A, P1D, P10C, P76A.
Row 5: K75A, K3C, K8D, K54A.

These five rows set the position of the pattern. Now follow the graph from here to Row 128. Commence use of optional lurex on Row 27. Adjust row counter to Row 152.
Row 153–200: Work in St.st.

Shape Shoulders
Row 201: Cast off 10sts. K to end of row.
Row 202: Cast off 10sts. P to end of row.
Row 203: Cast off 10sts. K to end of row.
Row 204: Cast off 10sts. P to end of row.
Row 205: Cast off 10sts. K to end of row.
Row 206: Cast off 10sts. P to end of row.
Row 207: Cast off 10sts. K to end of row.
Row 208: Cast off 10sts. P to end of row.

TURTLE NECK (front)
Continue on remaining 60sts for a further 40 rows in St.st. Cast off loosely.

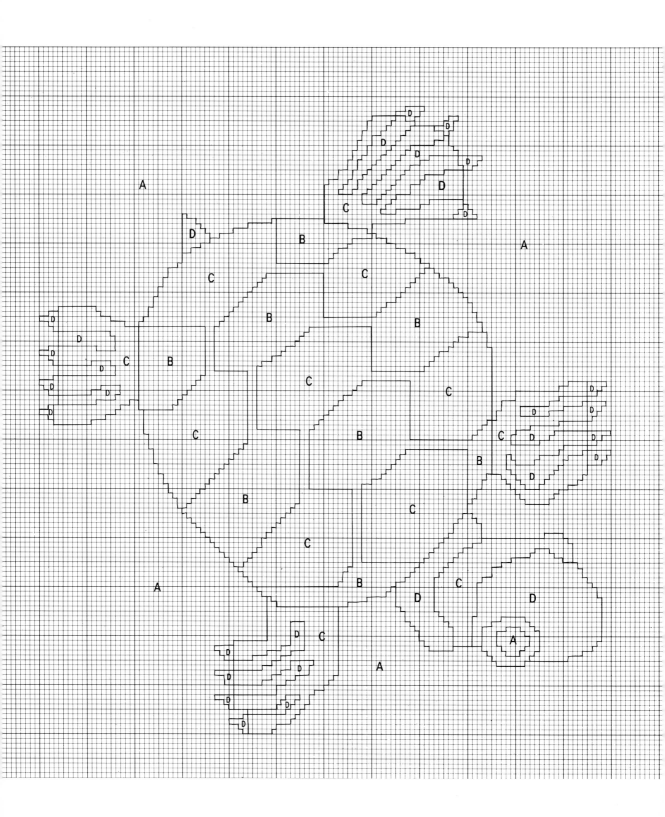

BACK

With colour A and 2¼mm (No.0) needles cast on 130sts. In single rib (K1,P1) work 30 rows.

Changing to 3¼mm (No.3) needles, K12, PU1, K12, PU1. Repeat 8 times, K10 (140sts).

Row 2–200: Work in St.st. starting with a P row.

Shape Shoulders

Row 201: Cast off 10sts. K to end of row.
Row 202: Cast off 10sts. P to end of row.
Row 203: Cast off 10sts. K to end of row.
Row 204: Cast off 10sts. P to end of row.
Row 205: Cast off 10sts. K to end of row.
Row 206: Cast off 10sts. P to end of row.
Row 207: Cast off 10sts. K to end of row.
Row 208: Cast off 10sts. P to end of row.

TURTLE NECK (back)

Continue on remaining 60sts for a further 40 rows in St.st. Cast off loosely.

SLEEVES (both alike)

With colour A and 2¼mm (No.0) needles cast on 66sts. In single rib (K1,P1) work 30 rows.

Changing to 3¼mm (No.3) needles, and working in St.st., increase one st. at both ends of the first row, the 4th row, the 8th row and every following 4th row until Row 124 (130sts).

Work 6 more rows in St.st. Cast off loosely.

EMBROIDERY

Refer to the chapter headed The Nature of the Beast, and embroider the eye and nostrils.

MAKING UP

Using the crochet hook, work the loose ends of the yarn through the back of several sts of their own colour, to secure. Do not make knots.

On a flat surface, carefully pin out to size and press each piece.

Do not press the ribbing.

Sew together the shoulder seams and neck seams, but leave open the last 3cm (2in). Turn sweater right side out, and carefully sew last 3cm (2in). When neck is rolled down, the seam will not show.

Find the centre of each sleeve top and line up with shoulder seam. Pin into place and sew, ensuring both armhole side seams are of equal length. Pin side and sleeve seams together and sew.

Press seams gently.

EAGLE & OWL

The Eagle struck me as an ideal sweater design for a man. I thought originally of spreading the wings across batwing sleeves, but then it occurred to me that men might not care much for that idea. So, you will be glad to know that, although this is not among the easier designs, I have at least saved you the agonies of having sleeves with gruesome complications. Those of you who have tackled the bat or the snake will be pleased!

I've embroidered around the beak and foot, because I thought it would be a lovely way of achieving a very specific shape, and of showing you how easy it is to embroider on knitted garments and to add all sorts of details. I was tempted to go mad and embroider feathers all over the place, which you could do if you wanted to add lots of detail and make the Eagle Sweater look really fascinating. Recently, for a calendar, I did some embroideries of birds, and they do lend themselves wonderfully to detailed stylizing of feathers and down; the sort of detail that is difficult to achieve in the knitting, but not hard, given time and patience, to add afterwards with embroidery. Chain stitch, as I've explained in the chapter The Nature of the Beast, is the most useful, but if you are an experienced embroiderer you can have endless fun adding feathers in, say, fishbone stitch or Vandyke stitch.

For those of you who loathe the thought of all that embroidery, I have shown with the Owl design that even my subtleties on the Eagle's foot and beak can be left out if you were to use gold lurex in order to give a stronger knitted outline. You will just have to cope with giving the birds their eyes, and I do think the talons add enormously to the excitement; so even if you shy away from the embroidery, do have patience and finish the birds off with the minimum amount of extra work.

The sweaters are being worn by George Chelley and his daughter, Abigail, who both enjoyed the idea of Beastly Subjects that look out of the ordinary. I wasn't too sure what the men were going to make of these sweaters, but without exception they loved them and felt perfectly happy wearing something a bit more daring than a pin-stripe suit.

97

INSTRUCTIONS: EAGLE

MATERIALS

18x20g Texere Yarns 50/50 silk/wool mix in Cream (No.1827)
1x20g each of Texere Yarns 50/50 silk/wool mix in Black (No.1813) and Yellow (No.1820)
1x50g Yarnworks silk/cotton in Light Brown (Taupe No.407)
1x25g Nina Miklin Vogue wool in Dark Brown (No.936)
1 reel Nina Miklin fine lurex in Gold
One pair each 3mm (No.2) and 3¾mm (No.4) knitting needles
One row counter
One stitch counter
One crochet hook

TENSION

26 stitches and 33 rows to 10cm x 10cm (4in) on size 3mm (No.2) needles in St.st. It is important that your tension sample measures exactly the above dimensions to ensure size of sweater. If you have less stitches use a smaller needle, if more stitches then use a larger needle.

MEASUREMENTS

Chest   117cm (46in)
Length   71cm (28in)
Sleeve seam   61cm (24in)

COLOUR CODING

The following instructions refer to the colours as shown here:
A Cream (background)
B Light Brown
C Dark Brown (with lurex)
D Black
E Yellow

PREPARATION

Divide the Black into four balls, the Yellow into four and the Dark Brown into two balls pre-wound with lurex (optional), but with three very small separate balls for the tufts on the leg. The Light Brown can be divided into three balls.

ABBREVIATIONS

K	knit.
P	purl.
st.	stitch.
sts	stitches.
St.st.	Stocking stitch, (one row knit, one row purl alternately).
inc.	increase one stitch by working twice into same stitch.
dec.	decrease by working 2 stitches together.
K2tog.	knit 2 stitches together.
P2tog.	purl 2 stitches together.
PU1	pick up the loop between the needles and place on left needle. Work this loop as an extra stitch.

FRONT

With colour A and 3mm (No.2) needles cast on 140sts. In single rib (K1,P1) work 30 rows.
Changing to 3¾mm (No.4) needles, K13, PU1, K13, PU1. Repeat 8 more times, finishing with K10 (150sts). Work 29 rows in St.st. starting with a P row.
Turn row counter to 0.

Start Pattern

Row 1: K37A, K11B, K27A, K5E, K29A, K5E, K36A.
Row 2: P36A, P5E, P29A, P5E, P27A, P12B, P36A.
Row 3: K34A, K15B, K26A, K5E, K19A, K7E, K3A, K5E, K36A.
Row 4: P36A, P5E, P2A, P9E, P18A, P5E, P26A, P17B, P32A.
Row 5: K30A, K20B, K25A, K4E, K18A, K4E, K4A, K9E, K36A.

These five rows set the position of the pattern. Now follow the graph from here to Row 148.
Adjust row counter to Row 178.
Row 179–190: Work in St.st.

Shape Neck

Row 191: K60, K2tog. Slip next 26sts on to the stitch holder. Join new colour A and K2tog. K60.
Row 192: P59, P2tog. On other side of neck P2tog. P59.
Repeat these two rows, decreasing one st. at both sides of neck edge, on the next 12 rows (48sts on either side).
Row 205–218: Work in St.st. on both sides of neck.

Shape Shoulders

Row 219: Cast off 16sts. K32. K other side of neck.
Row 220: Cast off 16sts. P32. P other side of neck.
Row 221: Cast off 16sts. K16. K other side of neck.
Row 222: Cast off 16sts. P16. P other side of neck.
Row 223: Cast off 16sts. K other side of neck.
Row 224: Cast off remaining 16sts.

FRONT NECK BAND

With colour A, 3mm (No.2) needles and right side facing, pick up and knit from top left-hand side of neck, 34sts. In single rib (K1,P1) work the 26sts from stitch holder. Then pick up and knit 34sts from the right side of neck. Work in single rib for a further 7 rows.
Cast off loosely in rib.

BACK

With colour A and 3mm (No.2) needles cast on 140sts. In single rib (K1,P1) work 30 rows.
Changing to 3¾mm (No.4) needles, K13, PU1, K13, PU1. Repeat 8 times, K10 (150sts).
Row 2-218: Work in St.st. starting with a P row.

Shape Shoulders

Row 219: Cast off 16sts. K to end of row.
Row 220: Cast off 16sts. P to end of row.
Row 221: Cast off 16sts. K to end of row.
Row 222: Cast off 16sts. P to end of row.
Row 223: Cast off 16sts. K to end of row.
Row 224: Cast off 16sts. P to end of row.

BACK NECK BAND

Changing to 3mm (No.2) needles, work 8 rows single rib on remaining 54sts.
Cast off loosely in rib.

SLEEVES (both alike)

With colour A and 3mm (No.2) needles cast on 66sts. In single rib (K1,P1) work 30 rows.
Changing to 3¾mm (No.4) needles, and working in St.st., increase one st. at both ends of the first row, the 4th row, the 8th row and every following 4th row until Row 150 (142sts).
Cast off loosely.

EMBROIDERY

Refer to the chapter headed The Nature of the Beast, and work embroidery.

MAKING UP

Using the crochet hook, work the loose ends of the yarn through the back of several sts of their own colour, to secure. Do not make knots.
On a flat surface, carefully pin out to size and press each piece.
Do not press the ribbing.
Sew together the shoulder seams. Find the centre of each sleeve top and line up with shoulder seam. Pin into place and sew, ensuring both armhole side seams are of equal length. Pin side and sleeve seams together and sew.
Press seams gently.

Instructions: Owl

MATERIALS

8x20g Texere Yarns 50/50 silk/wool mix in Red (No.1836)
1x20g Texere Yarns 50/50 silk/wool mix in Black (No.1813)
1x50g Yarnworks silk/cotton mix in Light Brown (Taupe No.407)
1x25g Nina Miklin Vogue wool in Dark Brown (No.936)
1 reel Patricia Roberts Gold lurex
One pair each 2¾mm (No.1) and 3¼mm (No.3) knitting needles
One row counter
One crochet hook

TENSION

26 stitches and 32 rows to 10cm x 10cm (4in) on size 3¼mm (No.3) needles in St.st. It is important that your tension sample measures exactly the above dimensions to ensure size of sweater. If you have less stitches use a smaller needle, if more stitches then use a larger needle.

MEASUREMENTS

Chest   101cm (40in)
Length   53cm (21in)

COLOUR CODING

The following instructions refer to the colours as shown here:
A Red (background)
B Light Brown
C Dark Brown
D Black
E Gold (lurex)

PREPARATION

Divide the Light Brown into two balls, the Dark Brown also into two balls, the Black into two, with three lengths of approximately 100cm (40in). The Gold lurex also needs to be cut into four long strands for the foot, and a separate small ball wound off for one eye.

ABBREVIATIONS

K   knit.
P   purl.
st.   stitch.
sts   stitches.
St.st. Stocking stitch, (one row knit, one row purl alternately).
inc.   increase one stitch by working into same stitch twice.
dec.   decrease by working 2 stitches together.
K2tog. knit 2 stitches together.
P2tog. purl 2 stitches together.
PU1   pick up the loop between the needles and place on left needle. Work this loop as an extra stitch.

FRONT

With colour A and 2¾mm (No.1) needles cast on 130sts. In single rib (K1,P1) work 25 rows.
Changing to 3¼mm (No.3) needles, K12, PU1, K12, PU1. Repeat 8 more times finishing with K10 (140sts).
Work one row P.
Turn row counter to 0.

Start Pattern

Row 1: K33A, K33B, K33A, K4E, K37A.
Row 2: P36A, P6E, P31A, P33B, P34A.
Row 3: K34A, K34B, K30A, K6E, K36A.
Row 4: P36A, P6E, P15A, P4E, P11A, P33B, P35A.

Row 5: K35A, K33B, K10A, K5E, K14A, K4E, K8A, K3E, K28A.

These five rows set the position of the pattern. Now follow the graph from here to Row 80.

Armhole Shaping

Row 81: Cast off 5sts. Continue to work pattern as set to end of row.
Row 82: Cast off 5sts. Continue to work pattern as set to end of row.
Row 83–110: Follow the graph as set (130sts).

Shape Neck

Row 111: K63A, K2tog. Join new colour A and K2tog. Work to end of row as graph.
Row 112: P64 as graph. On other side of neck P64.
Row 113: K62, K2tog. On other side of neck, K2tog. K to end as graph.
Row 114–142: Continue to shape V-neck by K2tog. on neck edge of every knit row, and completing pattern on Row 120.

Shape Shoulders

Row 143: Cast off 12sts. K35, K2tog. On other side of neck K2tog. K47.
Row 144: Cast off 12sts. P35. P other side of neck.
Row 145: Cast off 11sts. K23, K2tog. On other side of neck K2tog. K34.
Row 146: Cast off 11sts. P24. P other side of neck.
Row 147: Cast off 11sts. K10, K2tog. On other side of neck K2tog, K to end of row.
Row 148: Cast off 11sts. P12. P other side of neck.
Row 149: Cast off 9sts. Cast off last 2sts together. On

other side of neck, K2tog. K to end of row.

Row 150: Cast off remaining 11sts.

FRONT NECK BAND

With colour A, 2¾mm (No. 1) needles and right side facing, pick up and knit from top left-hand side of neck, 50sts. Work in single rib (K1, P1) for 7 rows, decreasing one st. (by K2tog.) at point of V as follows:

At end of Row 2, 4 and 6, K2tog.

At beginning of Row 3, 5 and 7, K2tog. (44sts).

Cast off loosely in rib.

Repeat for right-hand side of neck, but with wrong side facing, pick up and K50sts.

ARMHOLE RIB (both alike)

With right sides facing sew shoulder seams together. With colour A and 2¾mm (No. 1) needles pick up and knit 70sts on each side of shoulder seam.

In single rib (K1, P1) work 8 rows.

Cast off loosely in rib.

BACK

With colour A and 2¾mm (No. 1) needles cast on 130sts. In single rib (K1, P1) work 25 rows.

Changing to 3¾mm (No. 3) needles, K12, PU1, K12, PU1. Repeat 8 more times finishing with K10 (140sts).

Row 2–80: Work in St. st. starting with a P row.

Armhole Shaping

Row 81: Cast off 5sts. K to end of row.

Row 82: Cast off 5sts. P to end of row.

Row 83–142: Continue in St. st. (130sts).

Shape Shoulders

Row 143: Cast off 12sts. K to end of row.

Row 144: Cast off 12sts. P to end of row.

Row 145: Cast off 11sts. K to end of row.

Row 146: Cast off 11sts. P to end of row.

Row 147: Cast off 11sts. K to end of row.

Row 148: Cast off 11sts. P to end of row.

Row 149: Cast off 9sts. K to end of row.

Row 150: Cast off 9sts. P to end of row.

BACK NECK BAND

Changing to 2¾mm (No. 1) needles, work 8 rows single rib on remaining 44sts.

Cast off loosely in rib.

Insert armhole rib.

EMBROIDERY

Refer to the chapter headed The Nature of the Beast, and embroider the eyes and four claws.

MAKING UP

Using the crochet hook, work the loose ends of the yarn through the back of several sts of their own colour, to secure. Do not make knots.

Carefully sew together the ribbing at the point of V-neck, matching stitches. On a flat surface, pin out to size and press each piece. *Do not press the ribbing.* Pin and sew together the side seams and sew the ribbing carefully into the insert for the armhole shaping. Press the seams gently.

FROG

Gayle Hunnicutt makes anything she wears look glamorous, and I'm thrilled to have her in this book modelling the Frog Sweater.

As my friends are all well aware, one of my reasons for doing the book was my frog-collecting passion, and a desire to complete or at least add to the collection with a Frog Sweater. I've illustrated some of my favourite breeds of the real thing around this page – they have wonderful names like Lutz's Phyllomedusa, Darwin's Frog, Spring Peeper, Glass Frog, Bush Squeaker and Wallace's Flying Frog. The European Green Tree Frog has been the inspiration for this sweater.

It is a fairly difficult one to knit but not of the Real Brute type, and Anni Bowes, knitter extraordinaire, enjoyed working with the cotton. We have used cotton for quite a few of the sweaters: the colours available now are so beautiful and I suppose my main reason for choosing this kind of yarn is simply a personal preference. I'm slightly allergic to wool and find that cotton is just as warm in winter with a thermal vest underneath. I know people think of vests as rather unromantic and old-fashioned, but I must say I find them a great deal more romantic than a wool-induced rash!

The embroidery is a simple matter of a small circle of black chain stitch for the eye, highlighted (or is it highlit?) with one white chain stitch.

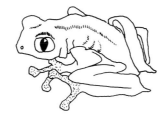

INSTRUCTIONS: FROG

MATERIALS
15x25g Patricia Roberts fine cotton in Khaki (No. 2)
1x25g each of Patricia Roberts fine cotton Green (No. 5), Pale Green (No. 22), Pink (No. 23), and Red (No. 6)
One pair each of 2¼mm (No. 0) and 3mm (No. 2) knitting needles
One row counter
One stitch holder
One crochet hook

TENSION
28 stitches and 36 rows to 10cm x 10cm (4in) on size 3mm (No. 2) needles in St. st. It is important that your tension sample measures exactly the above dimensions to ensure size of sweater. If you have less stitches use a smaller needle, if more stitches then use a larger needle.

MEASUREMENTS
Chest   104cm (41in)
Length   58cm (23in)
Sleeve seam   51cm (20in)

COLOUR CODING
The following instructions refer to the colours as shown here:
A Khaki (background)
B Green
C Pale Green
D Pink
E Red

PREPARATION
Divide the Green into six separate balls, the Pale Green into three and the Red into four balls. The Pink should be halved.

ABBREVIATIONS
K   knit.
P   purl.
st.   stitch.
sts   stitches.
St.st. Stocking stitch, (one row knit, one row purl alternately).
inc.   increase one stitch by working twice into same stitch.
dec.   decrease by working 2 stitches together.
K2tog. knit 2 stitches together.
P2tog. purl 2 stitches together.
PU1   pick up the loop between the needles and place on left needle. Work this loop as an extra stitch.

FRONT
With colour A and 2¼mm (No. 0) needles cast on 140sts. In single rib (K1, P1) work 30 rows.
Changing to 3mm (No. 2) needles, K13, PU1, K13, PU1. Repeat 8 more times, K10 (150sts).
Work 29 rows in St. st. starting with a P row.
Turn row counter to 0.

Start Pattern
Row 1: K39A, K6B, K105A.
Row 2: P104A, P9B, P37A.
Row 3: K36A, K12B, K102A.
Row 4: P97A, P17B, P36A.
Row 5: K36A, K21B, K26A, K14B, K53A.

These five rows set the position of the pattern. Now follow the graph from here to Row 121.
Adjust row counter to Row 151.
Row 152–164: Work in St. st.

Shape Neck
Row 165: K61, K2tog. Slip next 24sts on to the stitch holder. Join new colour A and K2tog. K61.
Row 166: P60, P2tog. On other side of neck, P2tog. P60.
Repeat these two rows, decreasing one st. at both sides of neck edge, on the next 8 rows (53sts on either side).
Row 175–186: Work in St. st. on both sides of neck.

Shape Shoulders
Row 187: Cast off 18sts. K35. K other side of neck.
Row 188: Cast off 18sts. P35. P other side of neck.
Row 189: Cast off 18sts. K17. K other side of neck.
Row 190: Cast off 18sts. P17. P other side of neck.
Row 191: Cast off 17sts. K other side of neck.
Row 192: Cast off remaining 17sts.

FRONT NECK BAND
With colour A, 2¼mm (No. 0) needles and right side facing, pick up and knit from top left-hand side of neck, 28sts. In single rib (K1, P1) work the 24sts from stitch holder. Then pick up and knit 28sts from the right side of neck. Work in single rib for a further 7 rows.
Cast off loosely in rib.

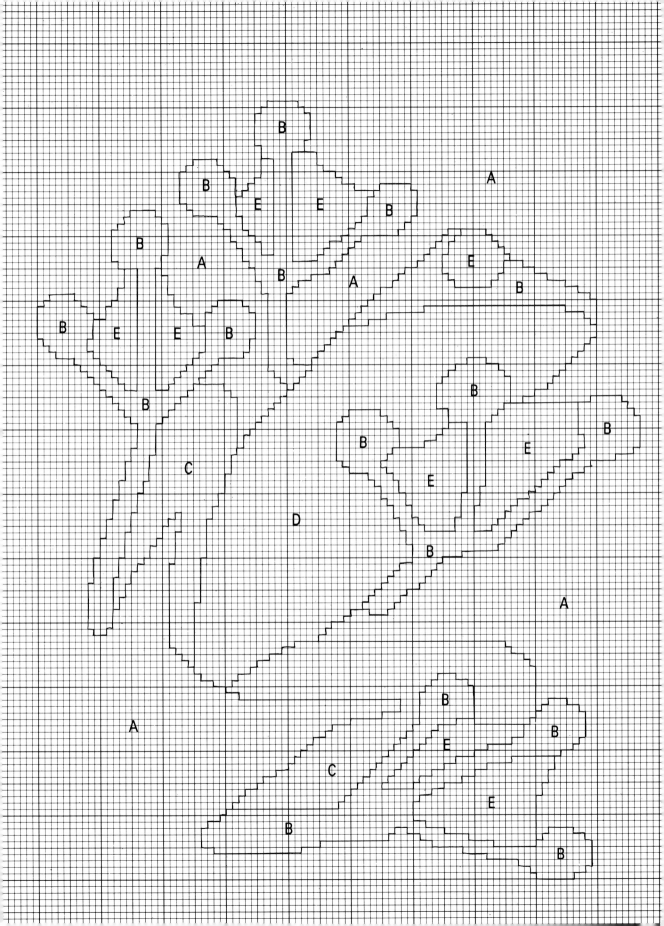

BACK

With colour A and 2¼mm (No. 0) needles cast on 140sts. In single rib (K1, P1) work 30 rows.
Changing to 3mm (No. 2) needles, K13, PU1, K13, PU1. Repeat 8 more times, K10 (150sts).
Row 2–186: Work in St. st. starting with a P row.

Shape Shoulders

Row 187: Cast off 18sts. K to end of row.
Row 188: Cast off 18sts. P to end of row.
Row 189: Cast off 18sts. K to end of row.
Row 190: Cast off 18sts. P to end of row.
Row 191: Cast off 17sts. K to end of row.
Row 192: Cast off 17sts. P to end of row.

BACK NECK BAND

Changing to 2¼mm (No. 0) needles, work 8 rows single rib on remaining 44sts.
Cast off loosely in rib.

SLEEVES (both alike)

With colour A and 2¼mm (No. 0) needles cast on 66sts. In single rib (K1, P1) work 30 rows.
Changing to 3mm (No. 2) needles, and working in St. st., increase one st. at both ends of the first row, the 3rd row, the 6th row and every following 3rd row until Row 130 (154sts).
Cast off loosely.

EMBROIDERY

Refer to the chapter headed The Nature of the Beast, and embroider the eye.

MAKING UP

Using the crochet hook, work the loose ends of the yarn through the back of several sts of their own colour, to secure. Do not make knots.
On a flat surface, carefully pin out to size and press each piece.
Do not press the ribbing.
Sew together the shoulder seams. Find the centre of each sleeve top and line up with shoulder seam. Pin into place and sew, ensuring both armhole side seams are of equal length. Pin side and sleeve seams together and sew.
Press seams gently.

TIGER & TIGER CUB

We decided to make the Tiger Cub sweater especially tiny because I was keen on the idea of a mother and small child wearing a tiger and its cub. Angela and Isabel Honour have proved my point by looking adorable in the Beastly Knits. It would have been difficult to imagine these sweaters shown off more perfectly, and Isabel, at fourteen months, proved a beautifully behaved model and seemed thoroughly to enjoy playing at being a tiger cub for the day. The only trouble was that she liked her sweater so much that she wanted to look at the design all the time, and a lot of pulling and wriggling went on to try to get around the difficulty of being inside the object of her attentions.

The Cub is somewhat easier to knit than its parent, mainly because the sweater is so much smaller and, of course, doesn't have any pattern on the back. We put buttons on the neckline, having made the sweater for such a small child, but obviously a larger size with a larger neckline won't need this detail. Neither of the sweaters is particularly easy, but they are not Real Brutes like the Lion, and you only have two colours to worry about, which is a help.

I've embroidered rather cartoon-like faces on both animals, but you could simplify them if you wanted to. Have a look at the chapter headed The Nature of the Beast, where I've explained how to do eyes and noses, and whiskers, and that sort of thing.

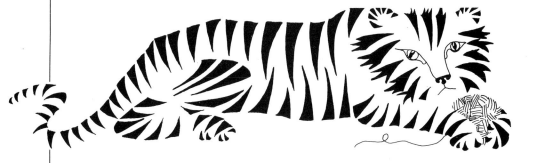

INSTRUCTIONS: TIGER

MATERIALS
17x25g Patricia Roberts fine cotton in Black (No.8)
2x25g Patricia Roberts fine cotton in Yellow (No.3)
One pair each 2¼mm (No.0) and 2¾mm (No.1) knitting needles
One row counter
One stitch holder
One crochet hook

TENSION
30 stitches and 38 rows to 10cm x 10cm (4in) on size 2¾mm (No.1) needles in St. st. It is important that your tension sample measures exactly the above dimensions to ensure size of sweater. If you have less stitches use a smaller needle, if more stitches use a larger needle.

MEASUREMENTS
Chest   101cm (40in)
Length   61cm (24in)
Sleeve seam   46cm (18in)

COLOUR CODING
The following instructions refer to the colours as shown here:
A Black
B Yellow

PREPARATION
Divide the Yellow into seven balls of various sizes.

ABBREVIATIONS
K   knit.
P   purl.
st.   stitch.
sts   stitches.
St.st. Stocking stitch, (one row knit, one row purl alternately).
inc.   increase one stitch by working into same stitch twice.
dec.   decrease by working 2 stitches together.
K2tog. knit 2 stitches together.
P2tog. purl 2 stitches together.
PU1   pick up the loop between the needles and place on left needle. Work this loop as an extra stitch.

FRONT
With colour A and 2¼mm (No.0) needles cast on 140sts. In single rib (K1, P1) work 30 rows.
Changing to 2¾mm (No.1) needles, K13, PU1, K13, PU1. Repeat 8 times, K10 (150sts).
Row 2–46: Work in St. st. starting with a P row.
Turn row counter to 0.

Start Pattern
Row 1: K65A, K4B, K81A.
Row 2: P81A, P7B, P62A.
Row 3: K62A, K7B, K18A, K4B, K63A.
Row 4: P58A, P9B, P14A, P11B, P62A.
Row 5: K61A, K12B, K14A, K9B, K58A.

These five rows set the position of the pattern. Now follow the graph from here to Row 94.
Turn row counter to Row 140.
Row 141–176: Work in St. st.

Shape Neck
Row 177: K61, K2tog. Slip next 24sts on to the stitch holder. Join new colour A and K2tog. K61.
Row 178: P60, P2tog. On other side of neck P2tog. P60.

Repeat these two rows, decreasing one st. at both sides of neck edge, on the next 12 rows (49sts on either side).
Row 191–200: Work in St. st. on both sides of neck.

Shape Shoulders
Row 201: Cast off 12sts. K37. K other side of neck.
Row 202: Cast off 12sts. P37. P other side of neck.
Row 203: Cast off 12sts. K25. K other side of neck.
Row 204: Cast off 12sts. P25. P other side of neck.
Row 205: Cast off 12sts. K13. K other side of neck.
Row 206: Cast off 12sts. P13. P other side of neck.
Row 207: Cast off 13sts. K other side of neck.
Row 208: Cast off remaining 13sts.

FRONT NECK BAND
With colour A, 2¼mm (No.0) needles and right side facing, pick up and knit from top left-hand side of neck, 32sts. In single rib (K1, P1) work the 24sts from stitch holder. Then pick up and knit 32sts from the right side of neck. Work in single rib for a further 7 rows.
Cast off loosely in rib.

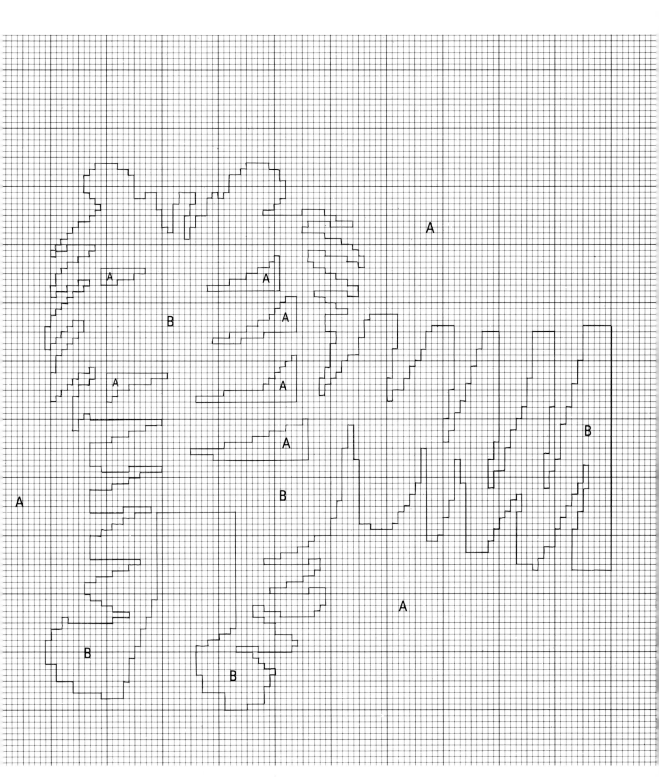

BACK

With colour A and 2¼mm (No. 0) needles cast on 140sts. In single rib (K1, P1) work 30 rows.

Changing to 2¾mm (No. 1) needles, K13, PU1, K13, PU1. Repeat 8 times, K10 (150sts).

Row 2–46: Work in St. st. starting with a P row.

Turn row counter to 0.

Start Pattern

Row 1: K97A, K5B, K48A.
Row 2: P47A, P9B, P94A.
Row 3: K91A, K12B, K47A.
Row 4: P43A, P17B, P90A.
Row 5: K86A, K20B, K44A.

These five rows set the position of the pattern. Now follow the graph from here to Row 68.

Turn row counter to Row 114.

Row 115–200: Work in St. st.

Shape Shoulders

Row 201: Cast off 12sts. K to end of row.
Row 202: Cast off 12sts. P to end of row.
Row 203: Cast off 12sts. K to end of row.
Row 204: Cast off 12sts. P to end of row.
Row 205: Cast off 12sts. K to end of row.
Row 206: Cast off 12sts. P to end of row.
Row 207: Cast off 13sts. K to end of row.
Row 208: Cast off 13sts. P to end of row.

BACK NECK BAND

Changing to 2¼mm (No. 0) needles, work 8 rows single rib on remaining 52sts.
Cast off loosely in rib.

SLEEVES (both alike)

With colour A and 2¼mm (No. 0) needles cast on 66sts. In single rib (K1, P1) work 30 rows.

Changing to 2¾mm (No. 1) needles, and working in St. st., increase one st. at both ends of the first row, the 4th row, the 8th row and every following 4th row until Row 130 (132sts).

Cast off loosely.

EMBROIDERY

Refer to the chapter headed The Nature of the Beast, and embroider the face and paws.

MAKING UP

Using the crochet hook, work the loose ends of the yarn through the back of several sts of their own colour, to secure. Do not make knots.

On a flat surface, carefully pin out to size and press each piece.

Do not press the ribbing.

Sew together the shoulder seams. Find the centre of each sleeve top and line up with shoulder seam. Pin into place and sew, ensuring both armhole side seams are of equal length. Pin side and sleeve seams together and sew.

Press seams gently.

114

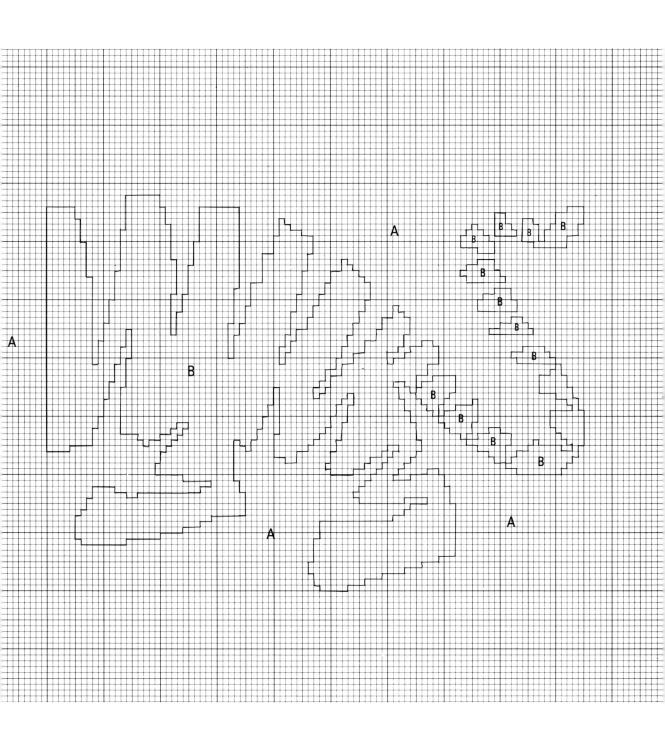

115

INSTRUCTIONS: TIGER CUB

MATERIALS

5x25g Patricia Roberts fine cotton in Black (No.8)
1x25g Patricia Roberts fine cotton in Yellow (No.3)
One pair each 2¼mm (No.0) and 2¾mm (No.1) knitting needles
Three black buttons 1½cm (⅝in) in diameter
One row counter
Two stitch holders
One crochet hook

TENSION

30 stitches and 38 rows to 10cm x 10cm (4in) on size 2¾mm (No.1) needles in St. st. It is important that your tension sample measures exactly above dimensions to ensure size of sweater. If you have less stitches use a smaller needle, if more stitches use a larger needle.

MEASUREMENTS

Chest	58cm (23in)
Length	31cm (12in)
Sleeve seam	24cm (9½in)

COLOUR CODING

The following instructions refer to the colours as shown here:
A Black
B Yellow

PREPARATION

Divide the Yellow into five small balls.

ABBREVIATIONS

K	knit.
P	purl.
st.	stitch.
sts	stitches.
St.st.	Stocking stitch, (one row knit, one row purl alternately).
inc.	increase one stitch by working into same stitch twice.
dec.	decrease by working 2 stitches together.
K2tog.	knit 2 stitches together.
P2tog.	purl 2 stitches together.

FRONT

With colour A and 2¼mm (No.0) needles cast on 90sts. In single rib (K1,P1) work 10 rows.
Changing to 2¾mm (No.1) needles work 30 rows in St. st. starting with a K row. Turn row counter to 0.

Start Pattern

Row 1: K21A, K4B, K65A.
Row 2: P60A, P9B, P21A.
Row 3: K18A, K12B, K20A, K4B, K36A.
Row 4: P32A, P12B, P13A, P15B, P18A.
Row 5: K18A, K15B, K13A, K12B, K32A.

These five rows set the position of the pattern. Now follow the graph from here to Row 60.
Adjust row counter to Row 90.
Row 91–110: Work in St. st.

Shape Neck

Row 111: K33, K2tog. Slip next 20sts on to the stitch holder. Join new colour A and K2tog. K33.
Row 112: P32, P2tog. On other side of neck P2tog. P32.
Repeat these two rows, decreasing one st. at both sides of neck edge, on the next 12 rows (21sts on either side).
Row 125–130: Work in St. st.

Row 131: Cast off 21sts on left-hand side of neck. Cast off 21sts on right-hand side of neck.

BACK

With colour A and 2¼mm (No.0) needles cast on 90sts. In single rib (K1,P1) work 10 rows.
Changing to 2¾mm (No.1) needles work 130 rows in St. st. starting with a K row.

Work Buttonholes

Row 131: Change to 2¼mm (No.0) needles and single rib 21sts. Turn work round.
Row 132: P1, K1, P1. Cast off 3sts. P1, K1, P1, K1, P1, K1. Cast off 3 sts. K1, P1, K1, P1, K1, P1. Turn work round.
Row 133: K1, P1, K1, P1, K1, P1. Turn work round and cast on 3sts. Turn work back and K1, P1, K1, P1, K1, P1, K1, P1, K1. Turn work round and cast on 3sts. Turn work back and P1, K1, P1, K1, P1, K1.
Row 134: Single rib 21sts starting with P1.
Row 135: Single rib 21sts starting with K1.
Row 136: Single rib 21sts starting with P1. Cast off 21sts in rib. Slip next 48sts on to the stitch holder. P21sts.
Row 137: Cast off 21sts.

NECK BAND

With right sides facing, sew left shoulder seams together. With colour A, 2¼mm (No.0) needles and right sides facing, pick up and knit from ribbing on back right shoulder, 6sts. Single rib (K1, P1) the 48sts across back from stitch holder.

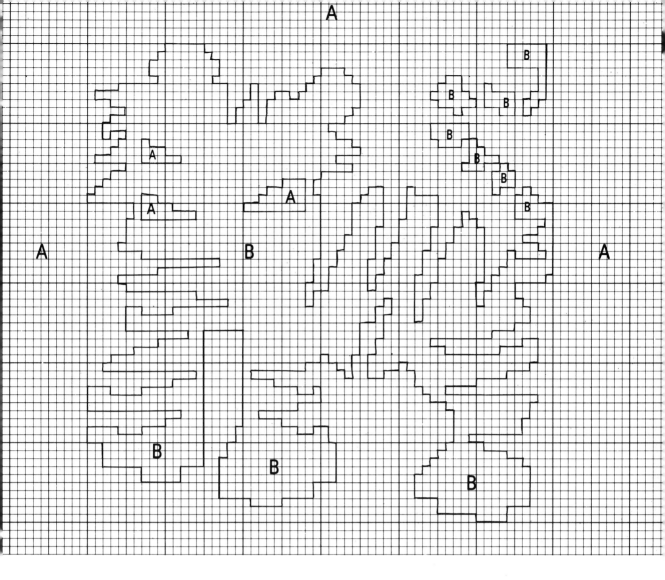

Then pick up and knit 20sts from left-hand side of neck. Single rib the 20sts across front from stitch holder, pick up and knit 20sts from right side of neck (114sts).
Row 2: Single rib 114sts.
Row 3: K1, P1, K1, P1. Cast off 3sts. P1, K1, P1 to end.
Row 4: K1, P1 to buttonhole. Turn work round and cast on 3sts. Turn work back and rib 7sts.
Rows 5 and 6: Work in single rib.
Cast off loosely in rib.

SLEEVES (both alike)
With colour A and 2¼mm (No.0) needles cast on 50sts.

In single rib work 25 rows. Changing to 2¾mm (No.1) needles, and working in St.st., increase one st. at both ends of the following 4th row, the 8th row and every following 4th row until Row 80 (90sts).
Cast off loosely.

EMBROIDERY
Refer to the chapter headed The Nature of the Beast, and embroider the face and paws.

MAKING UP
Using the crochet hook, work the loose ends of the yarn through the back of several sts of their own

colour, to secure. Do not make knots.
On a flat surface, carefully pin out to size and press each piece.
Do not press the ribbing.
Sew together the other shoulder seam. Find the centre of each sleeve top and line up with shoulder seam. Pin into place and sew, ensuring both armhole side seams are of equal length. Pin side and sleeve seams together and sew. Press seams gently. Sew on three buttons.

117

ELEPHANT

Gayle Hunnicutt's little boy, Edward Jenkins, is wearing a rather large Elephant Sweater. I thought since it was, after all, a large animal, it would be nice to make it in rather a large size for Edward, and he didn't seem to mind too much. I think he was more involved in riding my mother's beautiful fairground elephant.

The Elephant is medium-difficult to do, so follow the instructions carefully. I've given him silver toenails which I think make the sweater much more interesting. Make the outline of the nail in chain stitch, which is slightly tricky since the silver lurex does catch and snaggle easily, and then fill the nail with neat, horizontal stitches. Elephants are supposed to be distinguishable by the size of their ears – African elephants are the big-eared kind, and Asian elephants are the little-eared ones – but there are interesting differences in the numbers of toenails, too. It is so complicated that I shan't bore you with all the combinations of three on the back and four on the front of the African, or whatever the esoteric variations are. I'm sure you're not interested in elephants' toenails, so just do three on each foot, except for the back one where a single nail will do. You might be pleased to know that African and Indian elephants have two eyes each, and these are very easily embroidered with a semicircle of white chain stitch and a black French knot in the centre for each one. Oh yes, and I think, judging from the size of his ears, that this one must be African.

INSTRUCTIONS: ELEPHANT

MATERIALS
4x50g Jaeger alpaca in Pink (Fleur No. 307)
1x50g each of Jaeger alpaca in Light Grey (Paloma No. 148), Dark Grey (Plomo No. 149) and White (Arequipa No. 142)
1x25g Patricia Roberts fine cotton in Charcoal Grey
One pair each 2¼mm (No. 0) and 3mm (No. 2) knitting needles
One row counter
One stitch holder
One crochet hook

TENSION
26 stitches and 34 rows to 10cm x 10cm (4in) on size 3mm (No. 2) needles in St. st. It is important that your tension sample measures exactly the above dimensions to ensure size of sweater. If you have less stitches use a smaller needle, if more stitches then use a larger needle.

MEASUREMENTS
Chest	86cm (34in)
Length	54cm (17in)
Sleeve seam	33cm (13in)

COLOUR CODING
The following instructions refer to the colours as shown here:
A Pink (background)
B Light Grey
C Dark Grey
D Charcoal Grey
E White

PREPARATION
Divide the Light Grey into four equal balls, the Dark Grey into two balls, with a very small ball for the tail, the Charcoal Grey into three balls, the White into three balls.

ABBREVIATIONS
K	knit.
P	purl.
st.	stitch.
sts	stitches.
St. st.	Stocking stitch, (one row knit, one row purl alternately).
inc.	increase one stitch by working twice into same stitch.
dec.	decrease by working 2 stitches together.
K2tog.	knit 2 stitches together.
P2tog.	purl 2 stitches together.

FRONT
With colour A and 2¼mm (No. 0) needles cast on 120sts. In single rib (K1, P1) work 30 rows.
Changing to 3mm (No. 2) needles, work 10 rows in St. st., starting with a K row. Turn row counter to 0.

Start Pattern
Row 1: K20A, K13B, K17A, K19B, K21A, K12B, K18A.
Row 2: P18A, P13B, P19A, P21B, P16A, P14B, P19A.
Row 3: K18A, K15B, K16A, K22B, K17A, K14B, K18A.
Row 4: P18A, P15B, P16A, P22B, P16A, P16C, P17A.
Row 5: K16A, K17C, K16A, K22C, K15A, K16C, K18A.

These five rows set the position of the pattern. Now follow the graph from here to Row 94.
Adjust row counter to Row 104.
Row 105–110: Work in St. st.

Shape Neck
Row 111: K46, K2tog. Slip next 24sts on to the stitch holder. Join new colour A and K2tog. K46.
Row 112: P45, P2tog. On other side of neck P2tog. P45.
Repeat these two rows, decreasing one st. at both sides of neck edge, on the next 8 rows (38sts on either side).
Row 121–128: Work in St. st. on both sides of neck.

Shape Shoulders
Row 129: Cast off 13sts. K25. K other side of neck.
Row 130: Cast off 13sts. P25. P other side of neck.
Row 131: Cast off 13sts. K12. K other side of neck.
Row 132: Cast off 13sts. P12. P other side of neck.
Row 133: Cast off 12sts. K other side of neck.
Row 134: Cast off remaining 12sts.

FRONT NECK BAND
With colour A, 2¼mm (No. 0) needles and right side facing, pick up and knit from top left-hand side of neck, 24sts. In single rib (K1, P1) work the 24sts from stitch holder. Then pick up and knit 24sts from the right side of neck. Work in single rib for a further 7 rows.
Cast off loosely in rib.

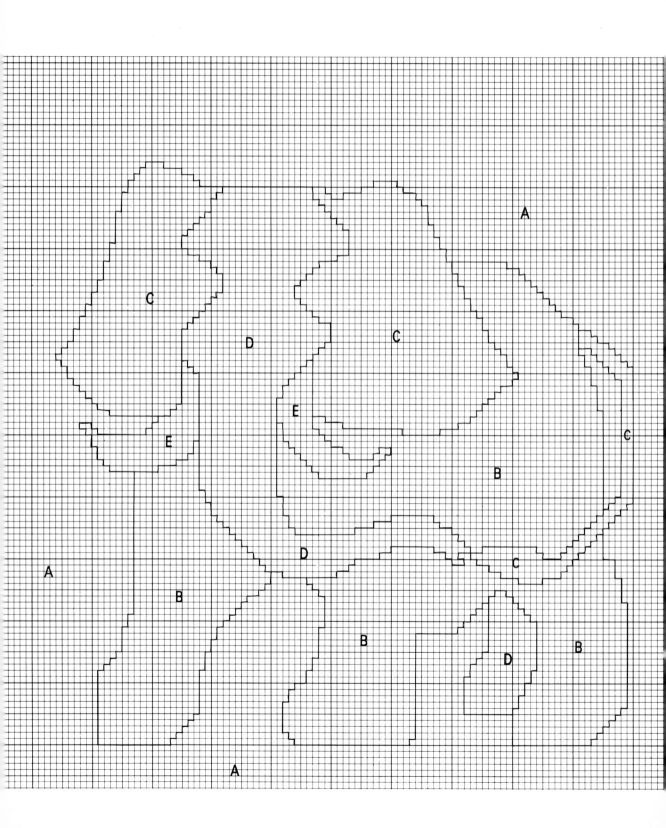

BACK

With colour A and 2¼mm (No.0) needles cast on 120sts. In single rib (K1,P1) work 30 rows.
Changing to 3mm (No.2) needles and starting with a K row, work 128 rows in St.st.

Shape Shoulders

Row 129: Cast off 13sts. K to end of row.
Row 130: Cast off 13sts. P to end of row.
Row 131: Cast off 13sts. K to end of row.
Row 132: Cast off 13sts. P to end of row.
Row 133: Cast off 12sts. K to end of row.
Row 134: Cast off 12sts. P to end of row.

BACK NECK BAND

Changing to 2¼mm (No.0) needles, work 8 rows single rib (K1,P1) on remaining 44sts.
Cast off loosely in rib.

SLEEVES (both alike)

With colour A and 2¼mm (No.0) needles cast on 60sts. Work 25 rows in single rib.
Changing to 3mm (No.2) needles, and working in St.st., increase one st. at both ends of the first row, the 4th row, the 8th row and every following 4th row until Row 76 (100sts).
Work 4 more rows in St.st. Cast off loosely.

EMBROIDERY

Refer to the chapter headed The Nature of the Beast, and embroider the eyes and toes.

MAKING UP

Using the crochet hook, work the loose ends of yarn through several sts of their own colour, to secure. Do not make knots.
On a flat surface, carefully pin out to size and press each piece.
Do not press the ribbing.
Sew together the shoulder seams. Find the centre of each sleeve top and line up with shoulder seam. Pin into place and sew, ensuring both armhole side seams are of equal length. Pin side and sleeve seams together and sew.
Press seams gently.

WHALE & FLAMINGO

I persuaded my father to wear the Whale, and I think it suits him very well. I wasn't going to let anyone else have the honour of sharing a photograph with him and, anyway, I wanted a good excuse to wear the Flamingo, which has always been one of my favourite birds. I remember watching a documentary about the flamingoes that gather in the Camargue in southern France, and they were just the most exquisite creatures ever. I love seeing them in flight, with their long, thin necks stretched out in front and their long, thin, knobbly-kneed legs stretched out behind.

I could hardly have designed a flying flamingo on a sweater, unless its head had started at one cuff, its neck went up the sleeve, joined the body in the middle, and its legs had gone down the other sleeve. And I would have looked rather silly with my arms stretched out all the time! So here it is, wrapped around my neck instead. Follow the instructions carefully. It's a medium-difficult sweater to knit, but so well worth it. I wore this one at a Dr Who convention in Chicago last year, and people were going mad with excitement about it. Everybody will think you look marvellous.

Everyone at the photo session thought that my father looked marvellous in the Whale, too. I was tempted, when embroidering the row of little silver teeth, to add one gold one, but the idea of a whale going to the dentist seemed a bit too ridiculous. I've used one single chain stitch in silver lurex for each tooth and I've chosen a brown colour to embroider the surround to his little flipper and along the pale grey edge of his jaw. The eye is made with a tiny circle of chain stitch and a white French knot in the middle. The eye should be placed exactly as it is in the photograph, just to one side of the flipper. We have followed the line of the V-neck with a fine spout of silver lurex, which is so subtle as to be hardly visible, but I think is rather a nice little optional extra. And, of course, although we have made this a sleeveless sweater, you can always have yourself a whale of a time making sleeves for a warmer version. The Flamingo needs an eye and a nostril: one chain stitch for the nostril, and an eye like the Whale's.

INSTRUCTIONS:WHALE

MATERIALS

7x25g Nina Miklin Vogue wool in White/Blue (No.940)
4x25g Patricia Roberts fine cotton in Charcoal Grey
1x25g Patricia Roberts fine cotton in Silver Grey
1 reel Nina Miklin fine lurex in Silver (optional)
One pair each 2¼mm (No.0) and 3¼mm (No.3) knitting needles
One row counter
One crochet hook

TENSION

26 stitches and 34 rows to 10cm x 10cm (4in) on size 3¼mm (No.3) needles in St.st. It is important that your tension sample measures exactly the above dimensions to ensure size of sweater. If you have less stitches use a smaller needle, if more stitches use a larger needle.

MEASUREMENTS

Chest   122cm (48in)
Length   69cm (27in)

COLOUR CODING

The following instructions refer to the colours as shown here:
A White/Blue (background)
B Charcoal Grey
C Silver Grey

PREPARATION

Divide the Silver Grey in half. If you decide to use the Silver lurex to define the water spout, you will need to pre-wind two small balls of the background colour (A) with the lurex. This is used 10sts either side of the V-neck shaping and although tiresome, does give a subtle effect. You will need to cross the yarns over when changing to the White/Blue alone in each row.

ABBREVIATIONS

K	knit.
P	purl.
st.	stitch.
sts	stitches.
St.st.	Stocking stitch, (one row knit, one row purl alternately).
inc.	increase by working into same stitch twice.
dec.	decrease by working 2 stitches together.
K2tog.	knit 2 stitches together.
P2tog.	purl 2 stitches together.
PU1	pick up the loop between the needles and place on left needle. Work this loop as an extra stitch.

FRONT

With colour A and 2¼mm (No.0) needles cast on 140sts. In single rib (K1,P1) work 30 rows.
Changing to 3¼mm (No.3) needles, K13, PU1, *K6, PU1. Repeat from * 18 times, K13 (160sts).
Row 2–50: Work in St.st. starting with a P row. Turn row counter to 0.

Start Pattern

Row 1: K101A, K8C, K51A.
Row 2: P50A, P10C, P100A.
Row 3: K100A, K11C, K49A.
Row 4: P40A, P9B, P12C, P49B, P50A.
Row 5: K50A, K49B, K12C, K10B, K39A.

These five rows set the position of the pattern. Now follow the graph from here to Row 89.

Armhole Shaping

Row 90: Cast off 5sts in colour B. Follow graph to end of row.
Row 91: Cast off 5sts in colour A. Follow graph to end of row.
Row 92–108: Follow graph. (If using the Silver lurex refer to Note at end of instructions). Adjust row counter to Row 158.
Row 159–168: Work in St.st.

Shape Neck

Row 169: P73, P2tog. Join new colour A and P2tog. P73.
Row 170: K72, K2tog. On other side of neck K2tog. K72.
Row 171: P to end.
Row 172–174: Dec. one st. at neck edge of next 2 rows. Work one row.
Repeat above 6 rows until Row 220.

Shape Shoulders

Continuing to dec. as above at neck edge, cast off 10sts at beginning (shoulder edge) of next 6 rows.
Row 227: Cast off 10sts. K other side of neck.
Row 228: Cast off remaining 10sts.

FRONT NECK BAND

With colour A, 2¼mm (No.0) needles and right side facing, pick up and knit from top left-hand side of neck, 60sts. Work in single rib (K1,P1) for 7 rows, decreasing one st. (by K2tog.) at point of V as follows:
At end of Row 3, 5 and 7, K2tog.

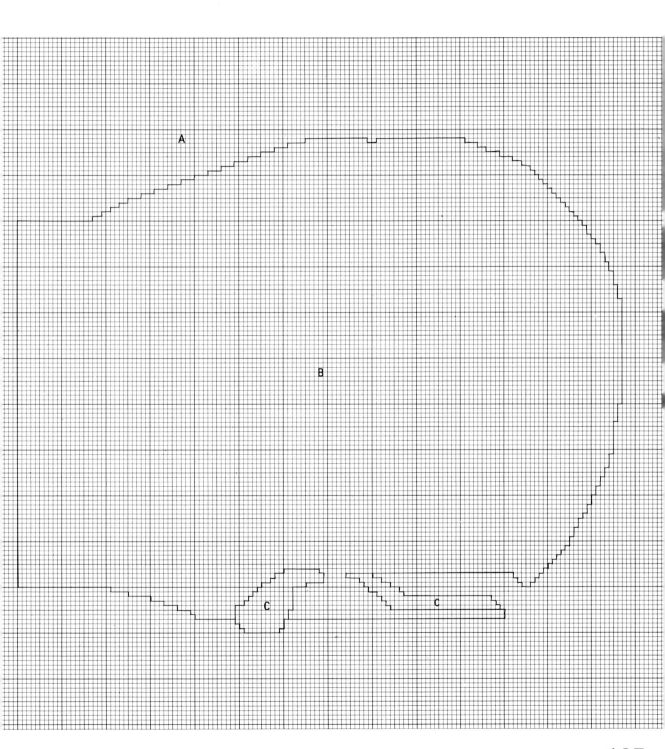

At beginning of Row 4 and 6, K2tog. (55sts).
Cast off loosely in rib.
Repeat for right-hand side of neck, but with wrong side facing, pick up and K60sts.

BACK

With colour A and 2¼mm (No.0) needles cast on 140sts. In single rib (K1,P1) work 30 rows.
Changing to 3¼mm (No.3) needles, K13, PU1, *K6, PU1. Repeat from * 18 times, K13 (160sts).
Row 2–60: Work in St.st. starting with a P row.
Turn row counter to 0.

Start Pattern

Row 1: K25B, K135A.
Row 2: P132A, P28B.
Row 3: K33B, K127A.
Row 4: P124A, P36B.
Row 5: K40B, K120A.

These five rows set the position of the pattern. Now follow the graph from here to Row 89.

Armhole Shaping

Row 90: Cast off 5sts in colour A. Follow graph to end of row.
Row 91: Cast off 5sts in colour B. Follow graph to end of row.
Row 92–116: Follow graph. Adjust row counter to Row 176.
Row 177–220: Work in St.st.

Shape Shoulders

Row 221: Cast off 10sts. K to end of row.
Row 222: Cast off 10sts. P to end of row.
Row 223: Cast off 10sts. K to end of row.
Row 224: Cast off 10sts. P to end of row.
Row 225: Cast off 10sts. K to end of row.
Row 226: Cast off 10sts. P to end of row.
Row 227: Cast off 10sts. K to end of row.
Row 228: Cast off 10sts. P to end of row.

BACK NECK BAND

Changing to 2¼mm (No.0) needles, work 8 rows single rib on remaining 80sts.
Cast off loosely in rib.

ARMHOLE RIBBING (both alike)

With right sides facing sew shoulder seams together. With colour A and 2¼mm (No.0) needles pick up and knit 60sts on each side of shoulder seam. In single rib (K1,P1) work 8 rows.
Cast off loosely in rib.

EMBROIDERY

Refer to the chapter headed The Nature of the Beast, and embroider the eye, teeth and fin outline.

MAKING UP

Using the crochet hook, work the loose ends of the yarn through the back of several sts of their own colour to secure. Do not make knots.
Carefully sew together the ribbing at the point of V neck, matching stitches.
On a flat surface, pin out to size and press each piece. *Do not press the ribbing.*
Pin and sew together the side seams and sew the ribbing carefully into the inset for the armhole shaping.
Press seams gently.

Optional Silver lurex

Start lurex at Row 159.
K73sts, join pre-wound A/lurex, K4sts, join new colour A (alone), K73.
Row 160: P72A, P6A/lurex, P72A.
Row 161: K71A, K8A/lurex, K71A.
Row 162–168: Continue to inc. one st. of A/lurex as above (22sts A/lurex).
Row 169: Follow pattern and join new A/lurex for other side of neck, losing one st. on neck shaping, leaving 10sts. either side of V neck.
Continue with 10sts either side to Row 228.

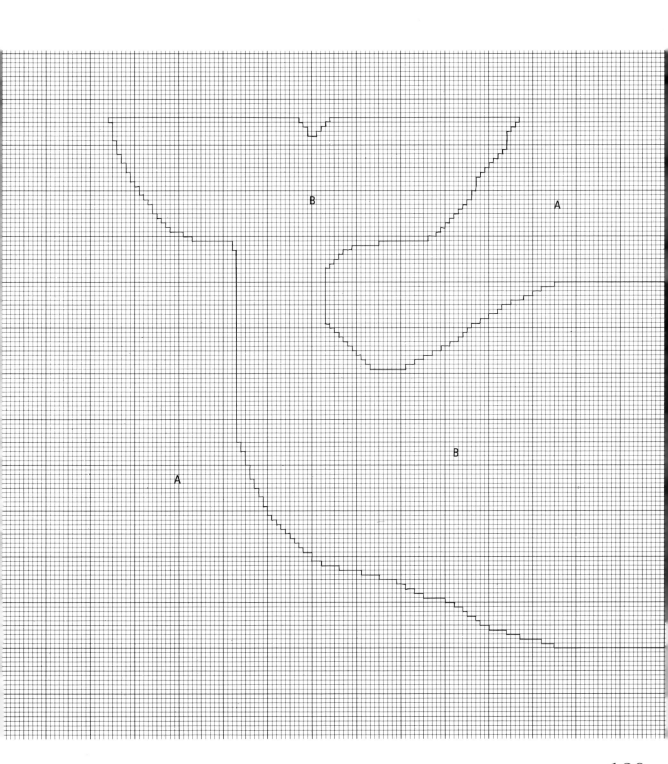

INSTRUCTIONS: FLAMINGO

MATERIALS
6x50g Yarnworks silk/cotton mix in Purple
1x50g Nina Miklin Ciocca cotton in Pink
1x20g Patricia Roberts angora in Dark Pink (Indien)
1x25g each Patricia Roberts fine cotton in Black (No.8) and Khaki (No.2)
1 reel Nina Miklin fine lurex in Pink (optional)
One pair each 2¼mm (No.0) and 3mm (No.2) knitting needles
One row counter
One stitch holder
One crochet hook

TENSION
24 stitches and 30 rows to 10cm x 10cm (4in) on size 3mm (No.2) needles in St.st. It is important that your tension sample measures exactly the above dimensions to ensure size of sweater. If you have less stitches use a smaller needle, if more stitches then use a larger needle.

MEASUREMENTS
Chest   107cm (42in)
Length   58cm (23in)
Sleeve seam   41cm (16in)

COLOUR CODING
The following instructions refer to the colours as shown here:
A Purple (background)
B Pink (cotton)
C Pink (angora)
D Black
E Khaki

PREPARATION
The feet and legs of the Flamingo are in double Pink cotton (using 2 strands). Therefore wind off six small balls in double yarn. The angora should have two very small balls for the top of the legs and the remainder pre-wound with the Pink lurex (optional) into three balls. The Khaki should be wound into four very small lengths for the feet and divide the remainder for the beak.

ABBREVIATIONS
K	knit.
P	purl.
st.	stitch.
sts	stitches.
St.st.	Stocking stitch, (one row knit, one row purl alternately).
inc.	increase one stitch by working same stitch twice.
dec.	decrease by working 2 stitches together.
K2tog.	knit 2 stitches together.
P2tog.	purl 2 stitches together.

FRONT
With colour A and 3mm (No.2) needles cast on 130sts.
Work 20 rows in St.st. starting with a K row.
Row 21: As you knit each st. pick up one st. at the back of the needle from the cast-on row, thus making a hem.
Row 22–26: Work in St.st. Turn row counter to 0.

Start Pattern
Row 1: K59A, K3B (doubled) K68A.
Row 2: P67A, P3B (doubled) P60A.
Row 3: K57A, K4E, K3B (doubled) K66A.
Row 4: P64A, P4B (doubled) P6E, P56A.

Row 5: K55A, K9E, K3B, (doubled), K24A, K2B (doubled), K37A.

These five rows set the position of the pattern. Now follow the graph from here to Row 156.

Shape Neck
Row 157: Still continuing to work the graph as set: K51, K2tog. Slip next 24sts on to the stitch holder. K2tog. K51.
Row 158: P50, P2tog. On other side of neck P2tog. P50.
Repeat these two rows, decreasing one st. at both sides of neck edge, on the next 12 rows (39sts on either side).
Row 171–180: Work in St.st. on both sides of neck.

Shape Shoulders
Row 181: Cast off 10sts. K29. K other side of neck.
Row 182: Cast off 10sts. P29. P other side of neck.
Row 183: Cast off 10sts. K19. K other side of neck.
Row 184: Cast off 10sts. P19. P other side of neck.
Row 185: Cast off 10sts. K9. K other side of neck.
Row 186: Cast off 10sts. P9. P other side of neck.
Row 187: Cast off 9sts. K other side of neck.
Row 188: Cast off remaining 9sts.

FRONT NECK BAND
With colour A, 2¼mm (No.0) needles and right side facing, pick up and knit from top left-hand side of neck, 32sts. In single rib (K1,P1) work the 24sts from stitch holder.

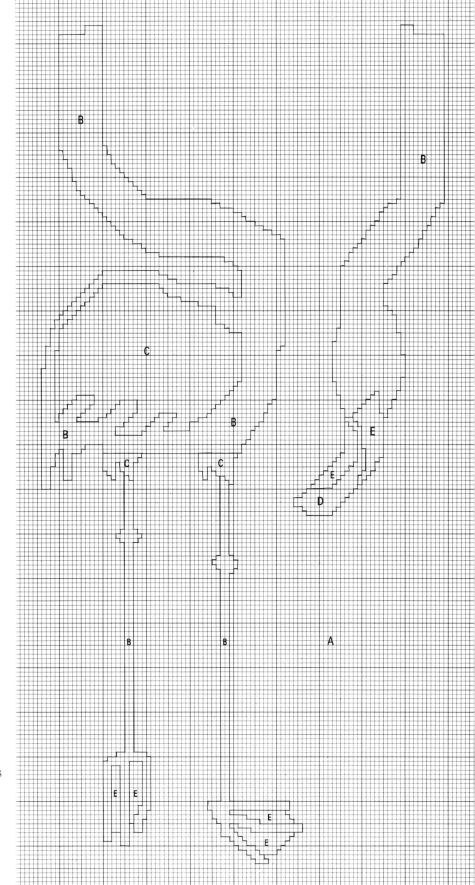

Then pick up and knit 32sts
from the right side of neck.
Work in single rib for a
further 7 rows.
Cast off loosely in rib.

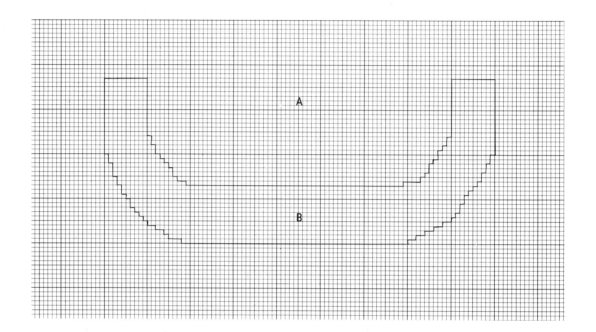

BACK
With colour A and 3mm (No.2) needles cast on 130sts.
Row 1–21: Work exactly as for Front.
Row 22–148: Work in St.st. Turn row counter to 0.

Start Pattern
Row 1: K40A, K52B, K38A.
Row 2: P35A, P57B, P38A.
Row 3: K36A, K60B, K34A.
Row 4: P32A, P64B, P34A.
Row 5: K32A, K68B, K30A.

These five rows set the position of the pattern. Now follow the graph from here to Row 32.
Turn row counter to Row 180.

Shape Shoulders
Row 181: Cast off 10sts. K to end of row.
Row 182: Cast off 10sts. P to end of row.

Row 183: Cast off 10sts. K to end of row.
Row 184: Cast off 10sts. P to end of row.
Row 185: Cast off 10sts. K to end of row.
Row 186: Cast off 10sts. P to end of row.
Row 187: Cast off 9sts. K to end of row.
Row 188: Cast off 9sts. P to end of row.

BACK NECK BAND
Changing to 2¼mm (No.0) needles, work 8 rows single rib on remaining 52sts.
Cast off loosely in rib.

SLEEVES (both alike)
With colour A and 3mm (No.2) needles cast on 110sts. Work 20 rows in St.st. starting with a K row.
Row 21: As you knit each st. pick up one st. at the back of the needle from the cast-on row, thus making a hem.

Row 22–130: Work in St.st. Cast off loosely.

EMBROIDERY
Refer to the chapter headed The Nature of the Beast, and embroider the eye.

MAKING UP
Using the crochet hook, work the loose ends of yarn through the back of several sts of their own colour, to secure. Do not make knots. On a flat surface, carefully pin out to size and press each piece.
Do not press the ribbing.
Sew together the shoulder seams. Find the centre of each sleeve top and line up with shoulder seam. Pin into place and sew, ensuring both armhole side seams are of equal length. Pin side and sleeve seams together and sew.
Press seams gently.

132

FOX & RABBIT

After a great deal of cajoling and wheedling, I finally persuaded our photographer, Colin Thomas, to wear the Fox Sweater. So I can now take up a few lines to say how superbly different he has made this book, and how patient and splendid he was to work with. Even in the face of opposition like the feline variety (see Jima Cat), he managed to stay calm and good-humoured throughout. On top of all that he has turned his hand to being equally successful on the other side of the camera, with a little help from a fairground rabbit and Suzy Ratner who is wearing the knitted Rabbit. Suzy liked the mixture of the soft angora and the cool cotton. The Fox's rust colour was very difficult to find, and I do think the very fine mohair that we eventually tracked down has worked beautifully. You will have to use it double to achieve the right thickness.

Any of these single designs could work just as well on the back of the sweater, if you wanted to be subtler about it. And, of course, if you were a real devil for punishment you could have the design on both the back and the front. It's entirely up to you.

The embroidery is simple, as usual (see the chapter headed The Nature of the Beast) and you will find the Rabbit among the easier sweaters to knit, while the Fox comes into the medium-difficult category.

133

INSTRUCTIONS: FOX

MATERIALS
8x50g Jaeger alpaca in Olive Green (No.383)
1x25g each of Nina Miklin fine mohair in Rust, Black and White
One pair each 2¼mm (No.0) and 3mm (No.2) knitting needles
One row counter
One crochet hook

TENSION
26 stitches and 34 rows to 10cm x 10cm (4in) on size 3mm (No.2) needles in St.st. It is important that your tension sample measures exactly the above dimensions to ensure size of sweater. If you have less stitches use a smaller needle, if more stitches use a larger needle.

MEASUREMENTS
Chest	117cm (46in)
Length	64cm (25in)
Sleeve seam	58cm (23in)

COLOUR CODING
The following instructions refer to the colours as shown here:
A Olive Green (background)
B Rust
C White
D Black

PREPARATION
Divide the Rust into four balls, the White into three balls and the Black into four long strands.

ABBREVIATIONS
K	knit.
P	purl.
st.	stitch.
sts	stitches.
St.st.	Stocking stitch, (one row knit, one row purl alternately).
inc.	increase by working into same stitch twice.
dec.	decrease by working 2 stitches together.
K2tog.	knit 2 stitches together.
P2tog.	purl 2 stitches together.
PU1	pick up the loop between the needles and place on left needle. Work this loop as an extra stitch.

FRONT
With colour A and 2¼mm (No.0) needles cast on 140sts. In single rib (K1,P1) work 30 rows.
Changing to 3mm (No.2) needles, K13, PU1, K13, PU1. Repeat 8 more times, K10 (150sts).
Work 79 rows in St.st. starting with a P row.
Turn row counter to 0.

Start Pattern
Row 1: K40A, K2C, K108A.
Row 2: P108A, P4C, P38A.
Row 3: K37A, K5C, K108A.
Row 4: P108A, P6C, P36A.
Row 5: K35A, K8C, K107A.

These five rows set the position of the pattern. Now follow the graph from here to Row 65.
Adjust row counter to Row 145.
Row 146–156: Work in St.st.

Shape Neck
Row 157: K73, K2tog. Join new colour A and K2tog. K73.
Row 158: P74 on both sides of neck.
Row 159: K72, K2tog. On other side of neck K2tog. K72.

Row 160: P73 on both sides of neck.
Row 161–226: Continue to dec. one st. at neck edge of every K row (40sts).

Shape Shoulders
Row 227: Still continuing to dec. as above on the neck edge, cast off 13sts. K to end of both sides.
Row 228: Cast off 13sts. P to end of both sides.
Row 229: Cast off 13sts. K to end of both sides.
Row 230: Cast off 13sts. P to end of both sides.
Row 231: Cast off 12sts. K other side of neck.
Row 232: Cast off remaining 11sts.

FRONT NECK BAND
With colour A, 2¼mm (No.0) needles and right side facing, pick up and knit from top left-hand side of neck, 76sts. Work in single rib (K1,P1) for 7 rows, decreasing one st. (by K2tog.) at point of V as follows:
At end of Row 3, 5 and 7, K2tog.
At beginning of Row 4 and 6, K2tog. (71sts).
Cast off loosely in rib.
Repeat for right-hand side of neck, but with wrong side facing, pick up and K76sts.

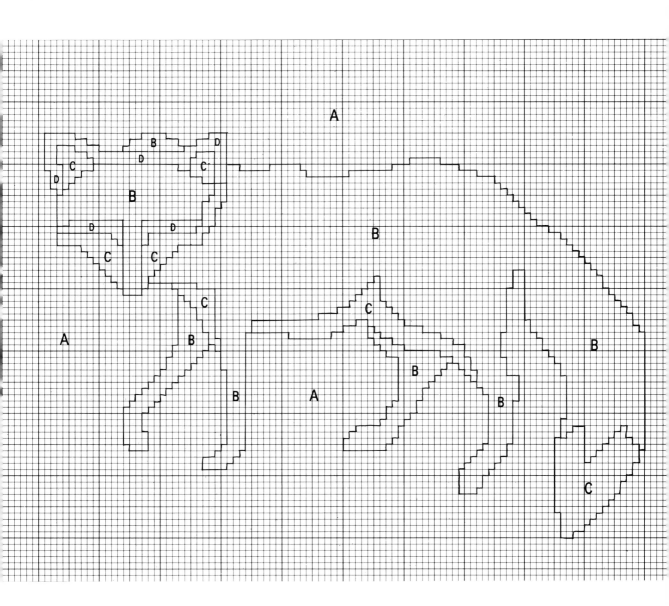

135

BACK

With colour A and 2¼mm (No. 0) needles cast on 140sts. In single rib (K1,P1) work 30 rows.
Changing to 3mm (No. 2) needles, K13, PU1, K13, PU1. Repeat 8 more times, K10 (150sts).
Row 2–226: Work in St. st. starting with a P row.

Shape Shoulders

Row 227: Cast off 13sts. K to end of row.
Row 228: Cast off 13sts. P to end of row.
Row 229: Cast off 13sts. K to end of row.
Row 230: Cast off 13sts. P to end of row.
Row 231: Cast off 12sts. K to end of row.
Row 232: Cast off 11sts. P to end of row.

BACK NECK BAND

Changing to 2¼mm (No. 0) needles, work 8 rows single rib on remaining 68sts.
Cast off loosely in rib.

SLEEVES (both alike)

With colour A and 2¼mm (No. 0) needles cast on 66sts.
In single rib work 30 rows.
Changing to 3mm (No. 2) needles, and working in St. st., increase one st. at both ends of the first row, the 4th row, the 8th row and every following 4th row until Row 156 (148sts).
Work 4 more rows in St. st. Cast off loosely.

EMBROIDERY

Refer to the chapter headed The Nature of the Beast, and embroider two eyes and the nose.

MAKING UP

Using the crochet hook, work the loose ends of the yarn through the back of several sts of their own colour, to secure. Do not make knots.
Carefully sew together the ribbing at the point of the V neck, matching stitches.
On a flat surface, carefully pin out to size and press each piece.
Do not press the ribbing.
Pin and sew together the shoulder seams. Find the centre of each sleeve top, line up with shoulder seam. Pin into place and sew, ensuring both armhole side seams are of equal length.
Pin side and sleeve seams together and sew.
Press seams gently.

Instructions: Rabbit

MATERIALS

11x25g Patricia Roberts fine cotton in Pink (No. 20)
1x20g each of Jaeger angora in White (No. 550) and Fawn (No. 557)
One pair each 2¼mm (No. 0) and 3mm (No. 2) knitting needles
One row counter
One stitch holder
One crochet hook

TENSION

28 stitches and 36 rows to 10cm x 10cm (4in) on size 3mm (No. 2) needles in St. st. It is important that your tension sample measures exactly the above dimensions to ensure size of sweater. If you have less stitches use a smaller needle, if more stitches then use a larger needle.

MEASUREMENTS

Chest	81cm (32in)
Length	48cm (19in)
Sleeve seam	43cm (17in)

COLOUR CODING

The following instructions refer to the colours as shown here:
A Pink (background)
B White
C Fawn

PREPARATION

Divide the Fawn and White into three balls each.

ABBREVIATIONS

K	knit.
P	purl.
st.	stitch.
sts	stitches.
St. st.	Stocking stitch, (one row knit, one row purl alternately).
inc.	increase one stitch by working same stitch twice.
dec.	decrease by working 2 stitches together.
K2tog.	knit 2 stitches together.
P2tog.	purl 2 stitches together.
PU1	pick up the loop between the needles and place on left needle. Work this loop as an extra stitch.

137

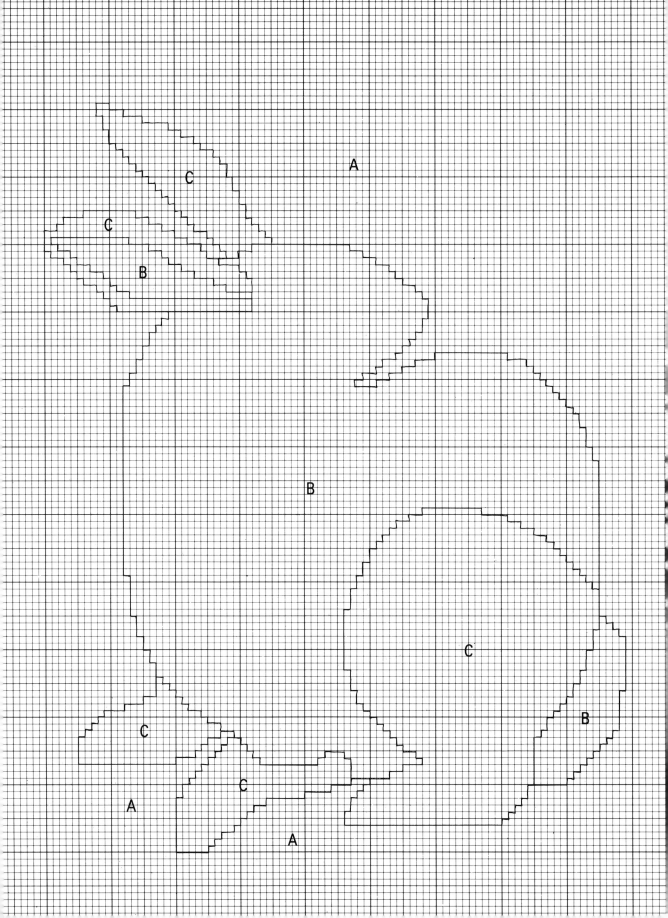

FRONT

With colour A and 2¼mm (No.0) needles cast on 110sts. In single rib (K1,P1) work 25 rows.
Changing to 3mm (No.2) needles K10, PU1, *K10, PU1. Repeat from * 8 times, K10 (120sts).
Row 2–10: Work in St.st. starting with a P row.
Turn row counter to 0.

Start Pattern

Row 1: K80A, K5C, K35A.
Row 2: P35A, P6C, P79A.
Row 3: K78A, K7C, K35A.
Row 4: P35A, P9C, P76A.
Row 5: K35A, K24C, K16A, K10C, K35A.

These five rows set the position of the pattern. Now follow the graph from here to Row 111.
Adjust row counter to Row 121.
Row 122–140: Work in St.st.

Shape Neck

Row 141: K46, K2tog. Slip next 24sts on to the stitch holder. Join new colour A and K2tog. K46.
Row 142: P45, P2tog. On other side of neck P2tog. P45.
Repeat these two rows, decreasing one st. at both sides of neck edge, on next 8 rows (38sts on either side).
Row 151–158: Work in St.st. on both sides of neck.

Shape Shoulders

Row 159: Cast off 12sts. K26. K other side of neck.
Row 160: Cast off 12sts. P26. P other side of neck.
Row 161: Cast off 12sts. K14. K other side of neck.

Row 162: Cast off 12sts. P14. P other side of neck.
Row 163: Cast off 14sts. K other side of neck.
Row 164: Cast off remaining 14sts.

FRONT NECK BAND

With colour A, 2¼mm (No.0) needles and right side facing, pick up and knit from top left-hand side of neck, 24sts. In single rib (K1,P1) work the 24sts from stitch holder. Then pick up and knit 24sts from the right side of neck. Work in single rib for a further 7 rows.
Cast off loosely in rib.

BACK

With colour A and 2¼mm (No.0) needles cast on 110sts. In single rib (K1,P1) work 25 rows.
Changing to 3mm (No.2) needles, K10, PU1, *K10, PU1. Repeat from * 8 times, K10 (120sts).
Row 2–158: Work in St.st. starting with a P row.

Shape Shoulders

Row 159: Cast off 12sts. K to end of row.
Row 160: Cast off 12sts. P to end of row.
Row 161: Cast off 12sts. K to end of row.
Row 162: Cast off 12sts. P to end of row.
Row 163: Cast off 14sts. K to end of row.
Row 164: Cast off 14sts. P to end of row.

BACK NECK BAND

Changing to 2¼mm (No.0) needles, work 8 rows single rib on remaining 44sts.
Cast off loosely in rib.

SLEEVES (both alike)

With colour A and 2¼mm (No.0) needles cast on 60sts. In single rib work 25 rows.
Changing to 3mm (No.2) needles, and working in St.st., increase one st. at both ends of the first row, the 4th row, 8th row and every following 4th row until Row 96 (110sts).
Work 4 more rows St.st.
Cast off loosely.

EMBROIDERY

Refer to the chapter headed The Nature of the Beast, and embroider the eye, nose and whiskers.

MAKING UP

Using the crochet hook, work the loose ends of the yarn through several sts of their own colour, to secure. Do not make knots.
On a flat surface, carefully pin out to size and press each piece.
Do not press the ribbing.
Sew together the shoulder seams. Find the centre of each sleeve top and line up with shoulder seam. Pin into place and sew, ensuring both armhole side seams are of equal length. Pin side and sleeve seams together and sew.
Press seams gently.

PENGUIN & CHICK

In this photograph the Penguin and its Chick look as if they are sitting on the table in front of Mirjana Bukvić-Winterbottom, who is modelling the sweater. Mirjana adored the softness of the silk/wool mixture, and there is something so lovely about this Penguin and its little angora Chick that, even though the sweater is fairly complicated to knit, it is still a pleasure because of the soft yarn and soothing subject matter. I discovered purely by chance, having asked Mirjana if she would wear one of my sweaters for the book, and thinking how good she would look in this one, that penguins are her favourite creatures and that I had chosen her favourite colours. Everyone who has seen it adores this sweater, so I hope you do too.

This is an Emperor penguin and it is the male that does all the baby-sitting. The female lays the egg and then disappears off to sea, leaving her mate to cope until the temperature gets warmer and the ice breaks. Then she comes back and takes over, giving him a chance to go off to get something to eat after sixty-four days of starving. Imagine! Once he gets his strength back, he comes back to help. Perhaps if you cook your man a really good dinner, he might take a turn at the knitting; you never know.

The embroidery is just a matter of an eye for the adult and one for the chick. A white French knot will do for the former, and a black one for the baby to highlight the pupils.

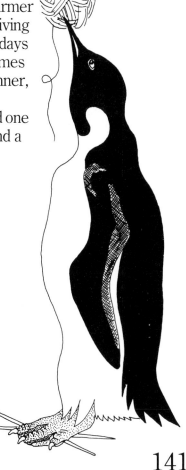

141

Instructions: Penguin & Chick

MATERIALS

17x20g Texere Yarns 50/50 silk/wool mix in Ice Grey (No.1823)

1x20g ball each Texere Yarns 50/50 silk/wool mix in Black (No.1813), White (No.1824), and Yellow (No.1820)

1x25g Patricia Roberts fine cotton in Charcoal Grey

1x20g each Patricia Roberts angora in Light Grey (Perl), and Dark Grey (Acier)

One pair each 3mm (No.2) and 3¾mm (No.4) knitting needles

One row counter

One stitch holder

One crochet hook

TENSION

26 stitches and 33 rows to 10cm x 10cm (4in) on size 3¾mm (No.4) needles in St.st. It is important that your tension sample measures exactly the above dimensions to ensure size of sweater. If you have less stitches use a smaller needle, if more stitches use a larger needle.

MEASUREMENTS

Chest	99cm (39in)
Length	58cm (23in)
Sleeve seam	56cm (22in)

COLOUR CODING

The following instructions refer to the colours as shown here:

A Ice Grey (background)
B Black
C White
D Yellow
E Charcoal Grey
F Light Grey
G Dark Grey

PREPARATION

Divide the Black into four separate balls, the White into four balls, the Yellow into two balls, the Charcoal into two balls and the Light Grey into two balls.

ABBREVIATIONS

K	knit.
P	purl.
st.	stitch.
sts	stitches.
St.st.	Stocking stitch, (one row knit, one row purl alternately).
inc.	increase by working into same stitch twice.
dec.	decrease by working 2 stitches together.
K2tog.	knit 2 stitches together.
P2tog.	purl 2 stitches together.
PU1	pick up the loop between the needles and place on left needle. Work this loop as an extra stitch.

FRONT

With colour A and 3mm (No.2) needles cast on 120sts. In single rib (K1,P1) work 30 rows.
Changing to 3¾mm (No.4) needles, K10, PU1, *K11, PU1. Repeat from * 8 times, K11 (130sts).
Work 24 rows in St.st. starting with a P row.
Turn row counter to 0.

Start Pattern

Row 1: P57A, P5E, P68A.
Row 2: K68A, K7E, K55A.
Row 3: P54A, P7E, P4A, P5E, P60A.

Row 4: K35A, K14E, K11F, K8E, K2A, K7E, K11A, K22B, K20A.
Row 5: P21A, P22B, P9A, P7E, P2A, P9E, P12F, P13E, P35A.

These five rows set the position of the pattern. Now follow the graph from here to Row 113.
Adjust row counter to Row 138.
Row 139–148: Work in St.st.

Shape Neck

Row 149: K51, K2tog. Slip next 24sts on to the stitch holder. Join new colour A and K2tog. K51.
Row 150: P50, P2tog. On other side of neck P2tog. P50.
Repeat these two rows, decreasing one st. at both sides of neck edge, on the next 10 rows (41sts on either side).
Row 161–172: Work in St.st. on both sides of neck.

Shape Shoulders

Row 173: Cast off 14sts. K27. K other side of neck.
Row 174: Cast off 14sts. P27. P other side of neck.
Row 175: Cast off 14sts. K13. K other side of neck.
Row 176: Cast off 14sts. P13. P other side of neck.
Row 177: Cast off 13sts. K other side of neck.
Row 178: Cast off remaining 13sts.

FRONT NECK BAND

With colour A, 3mm (No.2) needles and right side facing, pick up and knit from top left-hand side of neck, 30sts. In single rib (K1,P1) work the 24sts from stitch holder.

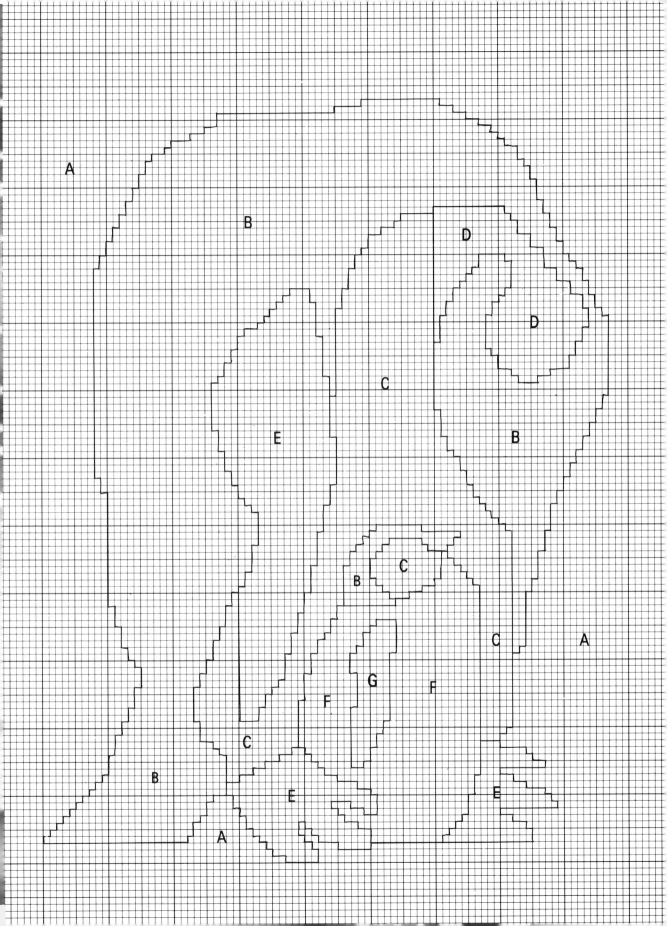

Then pick up and knit 30sts from right side of neck. Work in single rib for a further 7 rows.
Cast off loosely in rib.

BACK

With colour A and 3mm (No. 2) needles cast on 120sts. In single rib (K1, P1) work 30 rows.
Changing to 3¾mm (No. 4) needles, K10, PU1, *K11, PU1. Repeat from * 8 times, K11 (130sts).
Row 2–172: Work in St. st. starting with a P row.

Shape Shoulders

Row 173: Cast off 14sts. K to end of row.
Row 174: Cast off 14sts. P to end of row.
Row 175: Cast off 14sts. K to end of row.
Row 176: Cast off 14sts. P to end of row.
Row 177: Cast off 13sts. K to end of row.
Row 178: Cast off 13sts. P to end of row.

BACK NECK BAND

Changing to 3mm (No. 2) needles, work 8 rows single rib on remaining 48sts.
Cast off loosely.

SLEEVES (both alike)

With colour A and 3mm (No. 2) needles cast on 66sts. In single rib (K1, P1) work 30 rows.
Changing to 3¾mm (No. 4) needles, and working in St. st., increase one st. at both ends of the first row, the 4th row, the 8th row and every following 4th row until Row 130 (132sts).
Cast off loosely.

EMBROIDERY

Refer to the chapter headed The Nature of the Beast, and embroider both eyes.

MAKING UP

Using the crochet hook, work the loose ends of the yarn through the back of several sts of their own colour, to secure. Do not make knots.
On a flat surface, carefully pin out to size and press each piece.
Do not press the ribbing.
Pin and sew together the shoulder seams. Find the centre of each sleeve top and line up with shoulder seam. Pin into place and sew, ensuring both armhole side seams are of equal length. Pin side and sleeve seams together and sew.
Press seams gently.

DACHSHUND
& GOOSE (that laid the golden egg)

These sweaters are among the easiest to knit, and I think among
the most effective. They both make people laugh, especially if they
happen to have seen the backs first. A seemingly uninteresting
gold blob, and an equally unprepossessing black stripe; but when
the onlooker makes his way around to the other side, he finds a
somewhat surprised goose and either end of a sausage dog.

Anni Bowes and I thought we had better have one photograph
of us taken together, having amazed ourselves by remaining the
best of friends through all the ups and downs of endless technical
discussions, and the knots and tangles, difficulties and excitements
associated with working on a knitting book.

Yet again, you could if you wanted to use wool for the goose
and cotton for the dog. It's entirely up to you. I particularly liked
the wool and silk mixture that we have used on several of the
sweaters, because it is wonderfully soft and comfortable to wear.
There is very little embroidery needed to complete these two: just
a black circle of tiny chain or back stitch for the goose's eye and one
black chain stitch for the nostril on his beak. . . . I suppose I must
mean *her* beak, since she has just laid an egg. All the dachshund
needs is an eye. You could do the hooded, rather cartoon-style
sort of eye that I've embroidered on the tigers, or another simple
oval or circle with a single white stitch for the highlight.

So you see, these two really are lovely to do, and the goose
might just get the award for the easiest Beastly Knit. Maybe that
is because it's a bird and strictly speaking not beastly at all; except
that unfortunately the same (that is, the easiness) does not quite
apply to the other birds who have managed to sneak into this book.

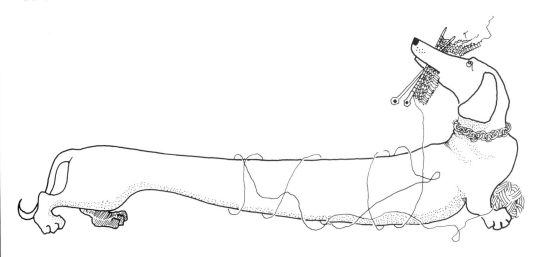

145

INSTRUCTIONS: DACHSHUND

MATERIALS

5x50g Jaeger alpaca in Vicuna (No.146)

1x50g each of Jaeger alpaca in Black (No.312) and Brown (Poncho No.145)

One pair each 2¼mm (No.0) and 3mm (No.2) knitting needles

One row counter

One stitch holder

One crochet hook

TENSION

26 stitches and 36 rows to 10cm x 10cm (4in) on size 3mm (No.2) needles in St.st. It is important that your tension sample measures exactly the above dimensions to ensure size of sweater. If you have less stitches use a smaller needle, if more stitches then use a larger needle.

MEASUREMENTS

Chest	101cm (40in)
Length	53cm (21in)
Sleeve seam	45cm (18in)

COLOUR CODING

The following instructions refer to the colours as shown here:

A Vicuna (background)

B Black

C Brown

PREPARATION

Divide the Black and Brown into six and three separate balls respectively.

ABBREVIATIONS

K	knit.
P	purl.
st.	stitch.
sts	stitches.
St.st.	Stocking stitch, (one row knit, one row purl alternately).
inc.	increase one stitch by working twice into the same stitch.
dec.	decrease by working 2 stitches together.
K2tog.	knit 2 stitches together.
P2tog.	purl 2 stitches together.
PU1	pick up the loop between the needles and place on left needle. Work this loop as an extra stitch.

FRONT

With colour A and 2¼mm (No.0) needles cast on 130sts. In single rib (K1,P1) work 30 rows.

Changing to 3mm (No.2) needles, K12, PU1, K12, PU1. Repeat 8 more times, finishing with K10 (140sts). Work 19 rows in St.st. starting with a P row.

Turn row counter to 0.

Start Pattern

Row 1: K30A, K11C, K49A, K12C, K38A.

Row 2: P37A, P14C, P47A, P13C, P29A.

Row 3: K28A, K15C, K43A, K18C, K36A.

Row 4: P35A, P20C, P41A, P17C, P6A, P10B, P11A.

Row 5: K10A, K12B, K5A, K18C, K38A, K23C, K34A.

These five rows set the position of the pattern. Now follow the graph from here to Row 101.

Adjust row counter to Row 121.

Row 122–140: Work in St.st.

Shape Neck

Row 141: K56, K2tog. Slip next 24sts on to the stitch holder. Join new colour A and K2tog. K56.

Row 142: P55, P2tog. On other side of neck P2tog. P55.

Repeat these two rows, decreasing one st. at both sides of neck edge, on the next 8 rows (48sts on either side).

Row 151–164: Work in St.st. on both sides of neck.

Shape Shoulders

Row 165: Cast off 12sts. K36. K other side of neck.

Row 166: Cast off 12sts. P36. P other side of neck.

Row 167: Cast off 12sts. K24. K other side of neck.

Row 168: Cast off 12sts. P24. P other side of neck.

Row 169: Cast off 12sts. K12. K other side of neck.

Row 170: Cast off 12sts. P12. P other side of neck.

Row 171: Cast off 12sts. K other side of neck.

Row 172: Cast off remaining 12sts.

FRONT NECK BAND

With colour A, 2¼mm (No.0) needles and right side facing, pick up and knit from top left-hand side of neck, 28sts. In single rib (K1,P1) work the 24sts from stitch holder. Then pick up and knit 28sts from the right side of neck. Work in single rib for a further 7 rows.

Cast off loosely in rib.

BACK

With colour A and 2¼mm (No.0) needles cast on 130sts. In single rib (K1,P1) work 30 rows.

Changing to 3mm (No.2) needles, K12, PU1, K12,

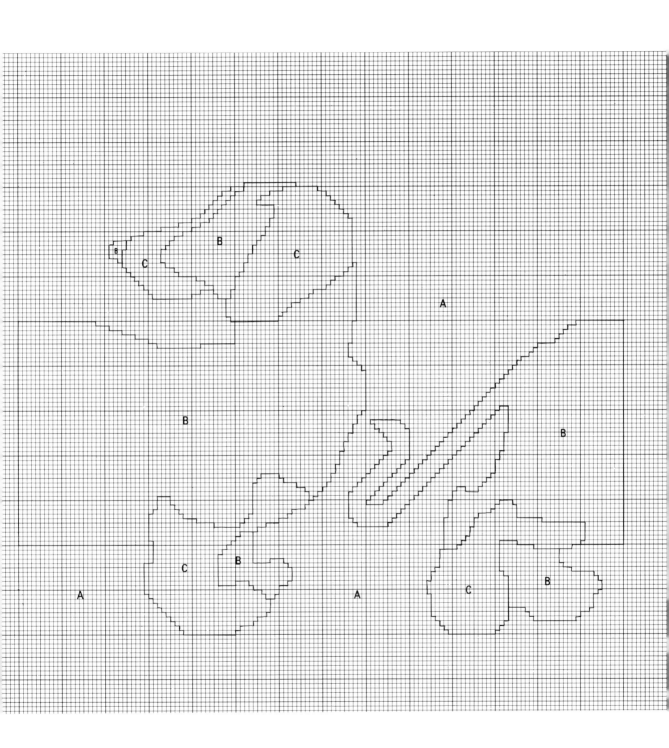

PU1. Repeat 8 times, K10 (140sts).
Row 2–40: Work in St. st. starting with a P row.
Row 41–90: Join colour B and work in St. st.
Row 91–164: Rejoin colour A and work in St. st.

Shape Shoulders

Row 165: Cast off 12sts. K to end of row.
Row 166: Cast off 12sts. P to end of row.
Row 167: Cast off 12sts. K to end of row.
Row 168: Cast off 12sts. P to end of row.
Row 169: Cast off 12sts. K to end of row.
Row 170: Cast off 12sts. P to end of row.
Row 171: Cast off 12sts. K to end of row.

Row 172: Cast off 12sts. P to end of row.

BACK NECK BAND

Changing to 2¼mm (No.0) needles, work 8 rows single rib on remaining 44sts.
Cast off loosely in rib.

SLEEVES (both alike)

With colour A and 2¼mm (No.0) needles cast on 60sts.
In single rib K1, P1 work 25 rows.
Changing to 3mm (No.2) needles, and working in St. st., increase one st. at both ends of the first row, the 4th row, the 8th row and every following 4th row until Row 116 (120sts).
Work a further 4 rows.
Cast off loosely.

EMBROIDERY

Refer to the chapter headed

The Nature of the Beast, and embroider the eye.

MAKING UP

Using the crochet hook, work the loose ends of the yarn through several sts of their own colour, to secure. Do not make knots.
On a flat surface, carefully pin out to size and press each piece.
Do not press the ribbing.
Sew together the shoulder seams. Find the centre of each sleeve top and line up with shoulder seam. Pin into place and sew, ensuring both armhole side seams are of equal length. Pin side and sleeve seams together and sew.
Press seams gently.

INSTRUCTIONS: GOOSE

MATERIALS

18x20g Texere Yarns 50/50 silk/wool mix in Black (No.1813)
2x20g Texere Yarns 50/50 silk/wool mix in White (No.1824)
1x25g Patricia Roberts fine cotton in Orange (No.21)
1 reel Patricia Roberts Gold lurex
One pair each 3mm (No.2) and 3¾mm (No.4) knitting needles
One row counter
One stitch holder
One crochet hook

TENSION

26 stitches and 33 rows to 10cm x 10cm (4in) on size 3¾mm (No.4) needles in St. st. It is important that

your tension sample measures exactly the above dimensions to ensure size of sweater. If you have less stitches use a smaller needle, if more stitches use a larger needle.

MEASUREMENTS

Chest 96cm (38in)
Length 61cm (24in)
Sleeve seam 51cm (20in)

COLOUR CODING

The following instructions refer to the colours as shown here:
A Black (background)
B White
C Orange
D Gold (lurex)

PREPARATION

Divide the Orange into two balls.

ABBREVIATIONS

K	knit.
P	purl.
st.	stitch.
sts	stitches.
St.st.	Stocking stitch, (one row knit, one row purl alternately).
inc.	increase by working same stitch twice.
dec.	decrease by working 2 stitches together.
K2tog.	knit 2 stitches together.
P2tog.	purl 2 stitches together.
PU1	pick up the loop between the needles and place on left needle. Work this loop as an extra stitch.

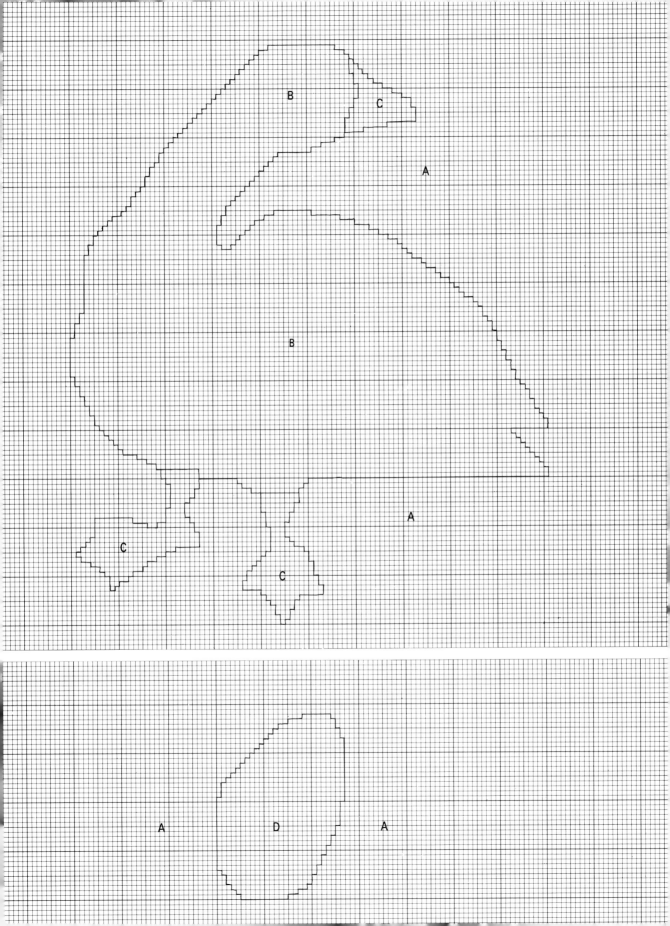

FRONT

With colour A and 3mm (No. 2) needles cast on 120sts. In single rib (K1, P1) work 30 rows.
Changing to 3¾mm (No. 4) needles K11, PU1, *K11, PU1. Repeat from * 8 times, K10 (130sts).
Row 2–25: Work in St. st. starting with a P row.
Turn row counter to 0.

Start Pattern

Row 1: P62A, P1C, P67A.
Row 2: K66A, K2C, K62A.
Row 3: P61A, P3C, P66A.
Row 4: K65A, K4C, K61A.
Row 5: P60A, P5C, P65A.

These five rows set the position of the pattern. Now follow the graph from here to Row 119.
Adjust row counter to Row 144.
Row 145–164: Work in St. st.

Shape Neck

Row 165: K51, K2tog. Slip next 24sts on to the stitch holder. Join new colour A and K2tog. K51.
Row 166: P50, P2tog. On other side of neck P2tog. P50.
Repeat these two rows, decreasing one st. at both sides of neck edge, on the next 8 rows (43sts on either side).
Row 175–184: Work in St. st. on both sides of neck.

Shape Shoulders

Row 185: Cast off 14sts. K29. K other side of neck.
Row 186: Cast off 14sts. P29. P other side of neck.
Row 187: Cast off 14sts. K15. K other side of neck.
Row 188: Cast off 14sts. P15. P other side of neck.
Row 189: Cast off 15sts. K other side of neck.
Row 190: Cast off remaining 15sts.

FRONT NECK BAND

With colour A, 3mm (No. 2) needles and right side facing, pick up and knit from top left-hand side of neck, 26sts. In single rib (K1, P1) work the 24sts from stitch holder. Then pick up and knit 26sts from the right side of neck. Work a further 7 rows in single rib.
Cast off loosely in rib.

BACK

With colour A and 3mm (No. 2) needles cast on 120sts. In single rib (K1, P1) work 30 rows.
Changing to 3¾mm (No. 4) needles K11, PU1, *K11, PU1. Repeat from * 8 times, K10 (130sts).
Row 2–25: Work in St. st. starting with a P row.
Turn row counter to 0.

Start Pattern

Row 1: P68A, P10D, P52A.
Row 2: K52A, K13D, K65A.

These two rows set the position of the pattern. Now follow the graph from here to Row 38.
Adjust row counter to Row 63.
Row 64–184: Work in St. st.

Shape Shoulders

Row 185: Cast off 14sts. K to end of row.
Row 186: Cast off 14sts. P to end of row.
Row 187: Cast off 14sts. K to end of row.
Row 188: Cast off 14sts. P to end of row.
Row 189: Cast off 15sts. K to end of row.
Row 190: Cast off 15sts. P to end of row.

BACK NECK BAND

Changing to 3mm (No. 2) needles, work 8 rows single rib on remaining 44sts.
Cast off loosely in rib.

SLEEVES (both alike)

With colour A and 3mm (No. 2) needles cast on 66sts. In single rib (K1, P1) work 30 rows.
Changing to 3¾mm (No. 4) needles, and working in St. st., increase one st. at both ends of the first row, the 4th row, the 8th row and every following 4th row until Row 130 (132sts).
Cast off loosely.

EMBROIDERY

Refer to the chapter headed The Nature of the Beast, and embroider the eye and the dot on the nose.

MAKING UP

Using the crochet hook, work the loose ends of the yarn through several sts of their own colour, to secure. Do not make knots.
On a flat surface, carefully pin out to size and press each piece.
Do not press the ribbing.
Sew together the shoulder seams. Find the centre of each sleeve top and line up with shoulder seam. Pin into place and sew, ensuring both armhole side seams are of equal length. Pin side and sleeve seams together and sew.
Press seams gently.

SNAKE

The other day I dug out some photographs of my brother and myself backstage in the Reptile House at the London Zoo, entwined from neck to ankle with boa constrictors and pythons. We got to know the head keeper in the Snake Department, Mr Landborne, and he used to let us get out the non-poisonous varieties, once they had had a good lunch and were disinclined to consume a couple of children for afters. I always get very cross when people say that snakes are slimy and disgusting. They are actually rather warm and comforting, as long as they don't give you too affectionate a hug. Perhaps a real live snake isn't quite as safe as a Snake Sweater, and Mr Landborne would certainly never have let us anywhere near the cobra on which this design is based, although we were allowed to poke the rattlesnakes with a long stick until they rattled their tails at us.

It's such a treat, after all the work involved in designing something as convoluted as this cobra, to have it modelled by someone as glamorous as my friend Sally Simpson. You may be reassured to know that it isn't quite such a snake in the grass to knit as it was to design. You will need to concentrate and follow the instructions carefully in order not to tie yourself in as many knots as I've made for the snake, but at least the embroidery is simple: a gold French knot for the eye and a gold forked tongue, which you can do in tiny chain stitch or in back stitch.

INSTRUCTIONS: SNAKE

MATERIALS

11x25g Nina Miklin Ciocca cotton in Orange
3x25g Patricia Roberts fine cotton in Black (No. 8)
2 reels Patricia Roberts Gold lurex
One pair each 2¾mm (No. 1) and 3¼mm (No. 3) knitting needles
One row counter
One stitch holder
One crochet hook

TENSION

26 stitches and 32 rows to 10cm x 10cm (4in) on size 3¼mm (No. 3) needles in St. st. It is important that your tension sample measures exactly the above dimensions to ensure size of sweater. If you have less stitches use a smaller needle, if more stitches use a larger needle.

MEASUREMENTS

Chest   107cm (42in)
Length   61cm (24in)
Sleeve seam 58cm (23in)

COLOUR CODING

The following instructions refer to the colours as shown here:
A Orange (background)
B Black
C Gold (lurex)

PREPARATION

Divide the Black balls in half, the Gold lurex into four balls.

ABBREVIATIONS

K   knit.
P   purl.
st.   stitch.
sts   stitches.
St.st. Stocking stitch, (one row knit, one row purl alternately).
inc.   increase one stitch by working same stitch twice.
dec.   decrease by working 2 stitches together.
K2tog. knit 2 stitches together.
P2tog. purl 2 stitches together.
PU1   pick up the loop between the needles and place on left needle. Work this loop as an extra stitch.

FRONT

With colour A and 2¾mm (No. 1) needles cast on 140sts. In single rib (K1, P1) work 30 rows.
Changing to 3¼mm (No. 3) needles, K13, PU1, K13, PU1. Repeat 8 more times, K10 (150sts).
Work 29 rows in St. st. starting with P row.
Turn row counter to 0.

Start Pattern

Row 1: K88A, K17B, K45A.
Row 2: P43A, P21B, P86A.
Row 3: K84A, K25B, K41A.
Row 4: P39A, P29B, P82A.
Row 5: K80A, K32B, K1C, K37A.

These five rows set the position of the pattern. Now follow the graph from here to Row 100.

Shape Neck

Row 101: Continuing to follow the graph as set, K73, K2tog. Join new colour A, and K2tog. K73. Now follow the graph for pattern and for neck shaping, decreasing one st. at both sides of neck where indicated, to Row 170 (43sts on either side).

Cast off loosely in appropriate colour.

FRONT NECK BAND

With colour A, 2¾mm (No. 1) needles and right side facing, pick up and knit from top left-hand side of neck, 70sts. Work in single rib (K1, P1) for 7 rows, decreasing one st. (by K2tog.) at point of V as follows:
At end of Row 3, 5 and 7, K2tog.
At beginning of Row 4 and 6, K2tog. (65sts).
Cast off loosely in rib.

Repeat for right-hand side of neck, but with wrong side facing, pick up and K70sts.

154

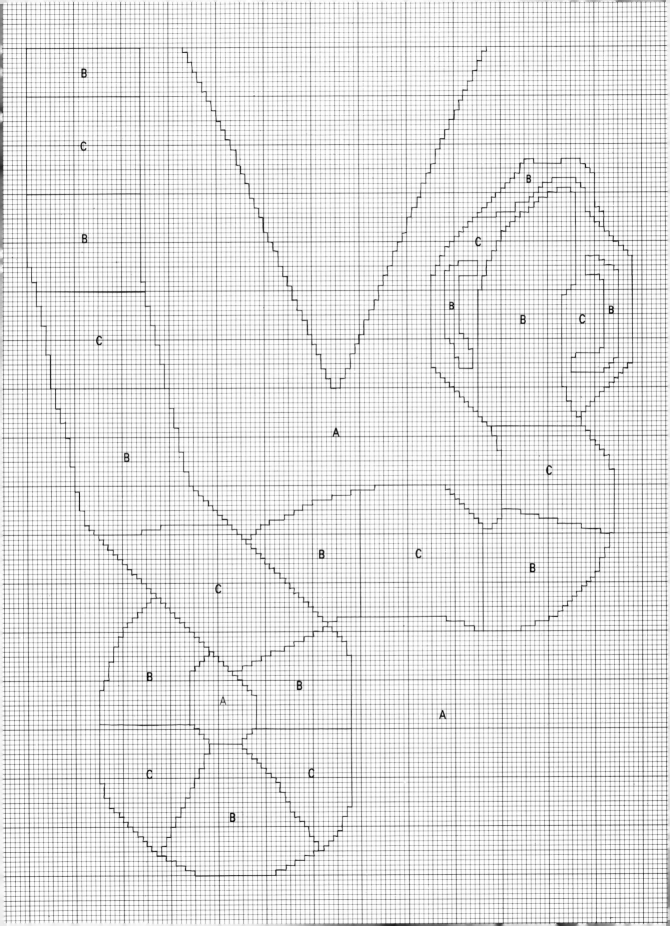

BACK

With colour A and 2¾mm (No. 1) needles cast on 140sts. In single rib work 30 rows.

Changing to 3¼mm (No. 3) needles, K13, PU1, K13, PU1. Repeat 8 more times, K10 (150sts).

Row 2-110: Work in St. st. starting with a P row.

Turn row counter to 0.

Start Pattern

Row 1: K55A, K15B, K27A, K3B, K10C, K40A.
Row 2: P35A, P15C, P6B, P22A, P2C, P19B, P51A.
Row 3: K48A, K21B, K5C, K18A, K8B, K18C, K32A.
Row 4: P29A, P21C, P11B, P13A, P8C, P23B, P45A.
Row 5: K43A, K24B, K11C, K9A, K13B, K22C, K28A.

These five rows set the position of the pattern. Now follow the graph from here to Row 90.

Cast off 43sts at beginning of next row and slip 64sts on to the stitch holder. Join new colour A and cast off remaining 43sts.

BACK NECK BAND

Changing to 2¾mm (No. 1) needles, work 8 rows on remaining 64sts from stitch holder in single rib (K1, P1). Cast off loosely in rib.

LEFT SLEEVE

With colour A and 2¾mm (No. 1) needles cast on 66sts. In single rib (K1, P1) work 30 rows.

Changing to 3¼mm (No. 3) needles, and working in St. st., increase one st. at both ends of the first row, the 4th row and every following

4th row as in the graph. At the same time follow the pattern as below:

Row 5: K53A, K2C, K8B, K7A.
Row 6: P5A, P10B, P6C, P49A.
Row 7: K47A, K8C, K11B, K4A.
Row 8: Inc. 1 into first st. K3A, K12B, K9C, K46A and inc. 1 into last st.

These four rows set the position of the pattern. Now follow the graph from here to Row 160, remembering to inc. one st. at both ends of every 4th row, and after row 110 where the outside edge continues off the graph (146sts).

NB: Do not increase on last row.

Cast off loosely.

RIGHT SLEEVE

With colour A and 2¾mm (No. 1) needles cast on 66sts. In single rib (K1, P1) work 30 rows.

Changing to 3¼mm (No. 3) needles, and working in St. st., increase one st. at both ends of the first row, the 4th row, the 8th row and every following 4th row until Row 159 (146sts).

Work one further row.

Cast off loosely.

EMBROIDERY

Refer to the chapter headed The Nature of the Beast, and embroider an eye and a forked tongue.

MAKING UP

Using the crochet hook work the loose ends of the yarn through the back of several

sts of their own colour, to secure. Do not make knots. On a flat surface, carefully pin out to size and press each piece.

Do not press the ribbing. Sew together the shoulder seams, lining up the pattern. Find the centre of each sleeve top and line up with shoulder seam. Pin into place and sew, ensuring both armhole side seams are of equal length. Pin side and sleeve seams together and sew.

Press seams gently.

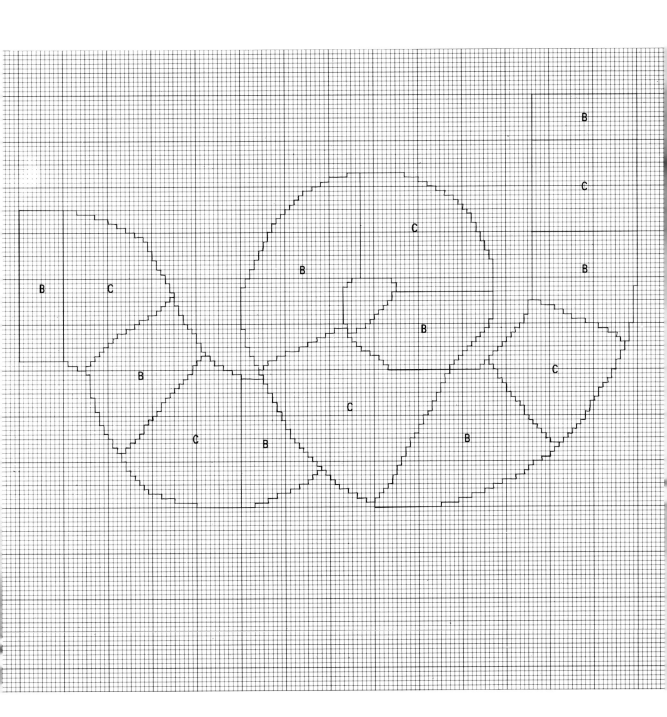

159

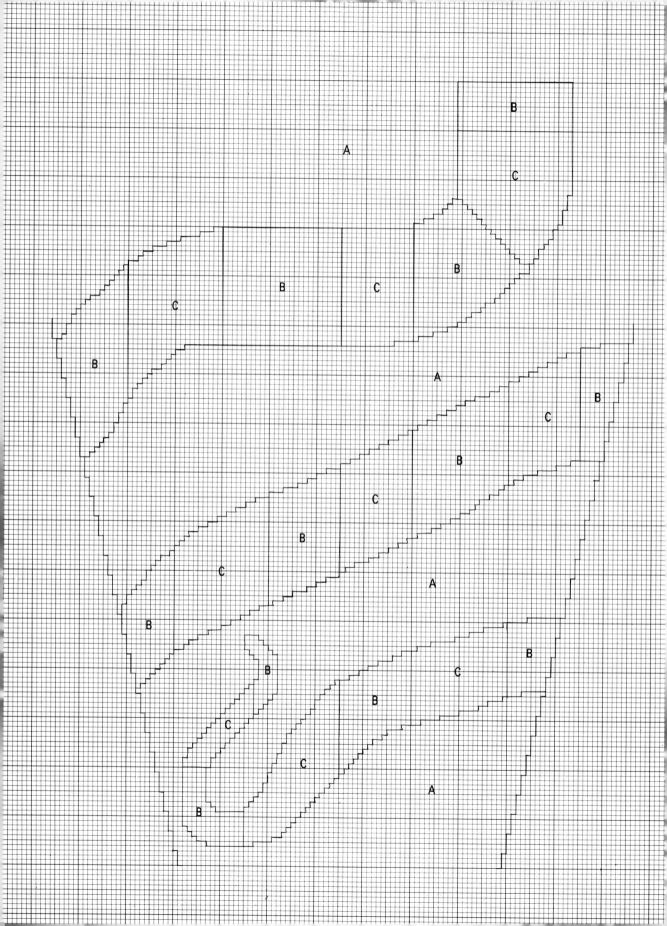